Sacrifice in Primal Religions

Christian Heritage Rediscovered

The Series, as the name suggests, is meant to focus on Christian Faith & Living vis-à-vis topics like Literature & Poetry, Indigenous Philosophizing, Ethical response towards Agriculture, Health & Healing, Science & Technology, Eco-feminist Theology, Sociological approach towards Human Rights, Law & Politics, Arts, History of Ideas, Ancient Civilizations, Cultural Contiguity, Religious Cosmologies & Mysticism, Footsteps of famous Theologians, World Peace & Harmony, Global Capitalism, Network Marketing, Cybertheology, Population & Demographics, Epigraphic Studies, Contextualized Education, and many others. We welcome a Mss. on any topic/s mentioned, whether they are original works, scholarly monographs, collections of conference papers, revised dissertations, or translations of historical documents. Through the Series we, the Publishers, are striving to put forward published works that may help Institutions, Academic Bodies, Researchers, Scholars and the World at large in furthering their respective knowledge and understanding on the concerned subject. We welcome your comments on our efforts and further suggestions on how we can foster the upcoming thought provoking theologically grounded books.

Christian Heritage Rediscovered - 74

Sacrifice in Primal Religions

Socio-economic & Religious Impacts and Role of the Church towards the Dimasa Kacharis of Assam

Lalchawiliana Varte

CWI

Christian World Imprints

First Published in 2019 by

Christian World Imprints
Christian Publishing & Books from India
H-12 Bali Nagar, **New Delhi-110015**
info@christianworldimprints.com
www.ChristianWorldImprints.com
Phone: +91 11 25465925

ISBN: 978-93-5148-336-6 (HB)
ISBN: 978-93-5148-337-3 (PB)

Printed in India.

DEDICATION

Dedicated to the memory
of my beloved father Elder Thantluanga Varte
who passed into glory on 25th June, 2016.

That the book in its original form is the thesis submitted to the Senate of Serampore College, towards the M.Th. degree and is published with written permission. The candidate is responsible for the title, contents and opinions expressed in it. The original title of the thesis is "The Impact of Sacrifices on the Socio-Economic and Religious Life of the Traditional Dimasa Kacharis in Dima Hasao District."

CONTENTS

PREFACE

The traditional Dimasa Kacharis of Dima Hasao in Assam, India, have their own religious heritage handed down orally from generation to generation. This traditional religion has managed to survive lively in the face of modernization and the influence of major religions. However, the huge amount of livestock and other sacrificial items makes these sacrifices very expensive. This research, therefore, attempts to determine the impact of sacrifices on the socio-economic and religious life of the traditional Dimasa Kacharis.

This book provides an anthropological overview of the traditional Dimasa Kacharis, giving a brief description of their social institutions, economic life and the traditional religious beliefs and concepts. Furthermore, in order to identify the importance of sacrifices in the traditional Dimasa Kachari religion, the various community and individual sacrifices of the traditional Dimasa Kacharis have been described, highlighting their purposes, the necessary preparations and the sacrificial rituals.

Employing the sociological method, this research ascertains the various impacts of sacrifice on the socio-economic and religious life of the traditional Dimasa Kacharis bringing to light the inter-relatedness between society and religion and the impact of religiosity on individuals and society. The findings highlight that the sacrifices are important as a cohesive factor binding the community together into a single moral community, preserving the valuable socio-cultural and religious heritages and also recognizing the practitioners their unique identity. Moreover, the book also highlights the negative impacts due to the expensiveness of the sacrifices and the rampant use of traditional rice beer. Consequently, the study acknowledge that sacrifices have negative as well as positive impacts upon the socio-economic and religious life of the Dimasa Kacharis.

Thus, attempt has been made to provide some suggestions and prospects for remedying the negative impacts of sacrifices without intruding upon the religious beliefs of the community. Further, a missiological challenge for the Church which has been involved in Christian mission for quite a long period of time among the Dimasa Kacharis towards a more effective holistic Christian mission which encompasses temporal and spiritual life has also been proposed.

I am incalculably indebted to those who have contributed variously for the materialization of this book. I take this opportunity to express my deep sense of gratefulness to my supervisor Prof. T. Vanlaltlani, whose astute guidance enabled me to complete the study. I am also indebted to Rev. Prof. V.S. Lalrinawma, HOD Department of Religions, Aizawl Theological College, for having kindly consented to write a foreword to this book.

I also am obliged to the Cachar Hill Tribes Synod for granting me permission to pursue my M.Th. studies. My overwhelming gratefulness is due to my family: My parents (L) Elder Thantluanga Varte and Mrs. Sangthuami, my sister Laltanpuii Varte, my wife Mrs. Lalsiamthari Varte and our three children David Vanlalhruaia Varte, Anna Lalremruati Varte and Noel Malsawmtluanga Varte, who have been beacons of light through the dark days and nights, pillars of strength in times when I needed support.

My special gratitude and appreciation also goes to Mr. Sudhanshu Kanda and his editorial team at Christian World Imprints, New Delhi, who undertook the meticulous editing work and publication of this book.

Ultimately, my gratitude goes to God who called me to His service, blessed me and guided me thus far. To Him alone be the Glory.

Lalchawiliana Varte

FOREWORD

It gives me a great pleasure to write foreword to the book entitled **"Sacrifice in Primal Religions: Socio-economic and Religious Impacts and Role of the Church towards the Dimasa Kacharis of Assam"**. The book is the product of a research done by Rev Lalchawiliana Varte who is presently teaching as an assistant professor at the Aizawl Theological College in the Department of Religions.

The fundamental concern of the book is to help readers to understand and identify the poor condition of the Dimasa Kachari Community, which is perhaps due to illiteracy and negligence by the Assam Government. The author has taken special care in highlighting the impacts that have been brought about by the animal sacrifices on the different aspects of life of the Dimasa Kachari Community of Dima Hasao District, with Haflong as its district headquarters. The Dimasa Kacharis believe that deaths, diseases and accidents are caused by the malevolent spirits and offering sacrifices of pigs, fowls, ducks and goats to appease them is must.

Despite a lot of criticism, animal sacrifices and other rituals serve as a cohesive factor binding the community into a single moral community and also provide them unity and strength to withstand outside forces. Moreover, these sacrificial rituals of the Dimasa Kacharis also have a deep ecological significance. This book will help the readers to understand that to do away with the negative impact of animal sacrifices upon the socio-economic and religious lives of the traditional Dimasa Kacharis, the rich tribal heritage and moral ethics have to be revived and reinterpreted by the educated Dimasa

Kacharis. In order to liberate this community from the enslavement of poverty, the rich tribal heritage must be revived and rediscovered. The Church which has been involved in Christian mission among the Dimasa Kacharis for many years also has a definite role to play in the socio-economic upliftment of the community and should be engaged more and more in a contextual and holistic mission. Therefore, the book may provide an opportunity for critical comments and discussion among scholars.

I personally know Rev. Lalchawiliana Varte from the very beginning of his theological journey at Aizawl Theological College Durtlang, Aizawl (Mizoram), and appreciate him for his scholarly work and sincerely hope that he will continue his interest in research which will be useful for students and scholars alike. I sincerely pray and hope that this creative and systematic research will increase the stock of knowledge about the poor condition of tribal communities in our nation and for making new schemes for their welfare. I wish that this book will be valued in every corner of our nation and abroad and will touch the hearts of every reader. I recommend the book to anyone who is interested to study tribal religion.

Rev. Prof. V.S. Lalrinawma
HOD, Department of Religions
Aizawl Theological College

Fig. 1: Map of Dima Hasao District

LIST OF TABLES

GLOSSARY

Bagaoba	:	community singing fellowship
Baiba Bdailaiba	:	singing and dancing competition during annual harvest festival
Bangfong	:	a bier made of split bamboo for carrying a corpse
Baroa	:	helper of a clan priest
Barwaju	:	assistant of a midwife
Busu	:	harvest festival
Busu Gaba	:	ceremonial blessing of youths by the elders
Daikho	:	abodes or unstructured shrines of area deities
Dainya	:	religious functionary who sacrifices the buffalo
Damra	:	heaven
Dilik	:	village herald
Disingba	:	marriage through negotiation
Dithar	:	holy water
Fangsla	:	artistic ceremonial gate made of split bamboo
Gajaibao	:	leader of annual harvest festival celebration
Garba	:	worship day or sacrificial day
Genna	:	restricted holiday

Gisia	highest religious leader
Gorashali	magician who can diagnose the cause of sicknesses
Gusu	impure
Hangseu	youth association
Hojai	village priest
Hojaijule	midwife
Hon	crushed rice
Julu/Jaddi	matriclan
Kalti	bride-price
Karma	a kind of stinging plant
Khalaima khamba	community feast during annual harvest festival
Khanaigusugarba	ceremonial shaving of a baby's hair
Khaolaba	marriage by mutual consent
Khapra	plate made of bamboo
Khilimphai	gifts given to priests
Khram	wooden traditional drum
Khram Dubong	musical instrument somewhat like the Jewish harp
Khunang	traditional headman
Krongfanggarba	village sacrifice for welfare, protection and good harvest
Lamphungba	ceremonial closing of village road
Langlai	deity invoked during pre-cultivation sacrifice
Laothaisa	bottle gourd pot used in offering rice beer
Longkhai	basket made of bamboo for carrying paddy
Madai	supreme god
Madaikhilimba	worship of clan deities
Madaikho	home of deities
Maimutharba	post-funeral sacrifice
Maisalaigarba	sacrifice for community welfare and good harvest

Majhai Khilingba	:	agricultural sacrifice
Makhamgarkhaoba	:	last offering of food and drink to the dead
Mangphlang	:	cremation ground
Mathlarao	:	female leader of the annual harvest festival celebration
Mayofagarba	:	sacrifice offered to all deities
Melphaiba	:	sacrificial feast during *Misengba*
Midogarba	:	sacramental meal/sacrifice offered at the time of marriage
Misengba	:	a community sacrifice which involves the entire Dimasa Kachari community
Misengba Melkhamba	:	*Misengba* Celebration Committee
Mi-staiba	:	slaughtering day of animals for feast
Misu	:	god's favour
Muree	:	a long wooden pipe consisting of three pieces
Muree Damyaba	:	musicians skilled in playing the traditional pipe
Muree-Wathesa	:	a trumpet produced from a special kind of bamboo tube
Nagahoja	:	male leader of the annual harvest festival celebration
Naijuni Khilimba	:	family sacrifice for development and prosperity
Naisodi-Nusodi	:	deity of child welfare
Nanadihangba	:	ceremonial bringing of new born baby outside the house
Nodrang	:	bachelor's dormitory
Phatri	:	diviner through whom deities speak
Rithar	:	traditional loincloth
Sakainjik	:	witches or female malevolent spirits
Sali	:	village council
Seng	:	sacrificial sword
Sengphong	:	patriclan
Sengphong Nimadai	:	worship of clan deity

Shaukhuli : clay figures made to represent the deities

Shupin : a kind of flute made of a small thin bamboo

Suba jiba : community feast in honour of *Gajaibao* and the *Hangseu*

Thaopari : lamp

Wadumaniba : a lesser sacrifice performed in lieu of *Misengba*

Zonthai : religious functionary of a particular clan

Zu : traditional rice beer

Chapter 1

THE RESEARCH PROBLEM AND METHODOLOGICAL CONSIDERATION

1. BACKGROUND OF THE RESEARCH

Sacrifice is the basic rite through which a religion performs its function in society. It has been found in religions all over the world. The traditional Dimasa Kacharis of Dima Hasao district which is in the state of Assam in India have their own religious heritage handed down orally from generation to generation. This traditional religion has managed to survive lively in the face of modernization and the influence of major religions. However, it appears that sacrifices have made both negative and positive impacts on different aspects of the traditional Dimasa Kachari life. This research, therefore, is an attempt to analyze the impact of the sacrifices on the socio-economic and religious life of the traditional Dimasa Kacharis.

2. AN ELABORATION

The Dimasa Kacharis have their own traditional religious heritage which is orally transmitted. In spite of the influence of Hinduism, Christianity and other religious faiths on the Dimasa Kacharis of rural Dima Hasao[1] district, they continue to hold on to their traditional religion.

The term 'sacrifice' originated from the Latin word *Sacrificium* where *sacer* means "holy", while *facere* means "to make". Thus, sacrifice means "to make holy". It "carries the connotation of the religious act in the highest or fullest sense; it can also be understood as the act of sanctifying or consecrating an object."[2] Sacrifice generally refers to "an offering, e.g., of animal life, food or incense, made to a deity, etc., as propitiation, thanksgiving etc."[3] Hence, sacrifice is the religious act of making holy an animal, food or incense offered to a deity as propitiation or thanksgiving etc.

Due to their belief in the existence of benevolent and malevolent spirits, sacrifice occupies a prominent place in the traditional Dimasa Kacharis religion and it is called '*bandai*'. This term especially refers to the sacrifice of blood to the deities or spirits and carries the connotation of a gift or an offering of thanksgiving or appeasement. Since sacrifice assumes an important position in the Dimasa Kachari religion, it necessitates the tracing of the origin of sacrifice.

The various sacrifices of the traditional Dimasa Kacharis of Dima Hasao district may be broadly classified into community sacrifices and individual sacrifices.[4] In the traditional Dimasa Kachari religion, sacrifice is a means of propitiation as well as thanksgiving. Moreover, as asserted by Chatry, sacrifices are offered not only for the

---

[1] Dima Hasao district is an administrative district in the state of Assam, with Haflong as its district headquarters. Dima Hasao district occupies an area of 4,888 sq. kms. It is the third largest district of Assam. According to the 2011 census, Dima Hasao district had a population of 214,102 and a literacy rate of 77.54%. See "Dima Hasao district," http://www.indianetzone.com/57/dima_hasao_district.htm (5 July 2013); "Dima Hasao," http://www.census2011.co.in/census/district/150-dima-hasao.html (2 July 2013).

[2] Joseph Henninger, "Sacrifice," *The Encyclopedia of Religion*, edited by Mircea Eliade, vol. 12 (New York: Macmillan Publishing Company, 1987), 544-557.

[3] "Sacrifice," *New Webster's Dictionary and Thesaurus of the English Language,* edited by Donald O. Bolander, et. al. (Danbury, CT: Lexicon Publications, Inc., 1992), 876.

[4] In the course of this study, community is used to refer to the entire Dimasa Kachari community and the community of a particular village, a particular area or a particular clan. Whereas, individual refers to an individual person or a family.

appeasement of spiritual beings, but also to the land; for its purity and to make it productive and bear abundant fruit.[5]

The majority of the Dimasa Kacharis living in the rural areas depend on agriculture for their livelihood.[6] They are people who are struggling to have two square meals a day. The huge amount of livestock and materials demanded by the sacrifices may have a negative impact on the economy of the people though it seems to give them spiritual nourishment. The various religious sacrifices have led them to economic depravity.

In the face of the influence of Hinduism, Christianity and other religious faiths, the traditional Dimasa Kacharis of rural Dima Hasao district have held on to their traditional religious beliefs and practices. As asserted by T. Vanlaltlani in the case of the Bru of Mizoram, so also in the case of the traditional Dimasa Kacharis it is perfectly true to state that, "the significant and essential values of such a stable religious identity deserve a deeper probe and careful analysis".[7] In this connection, the religious rites and rituals especially the sacrifices seem to be the backbone of their religious identity and what binds them together as community. This on the other hand may be considered to be a positive impact of the sacrifices. Therefore, an in-depth study of their sacrificial rituals will be noteworthy.

3. IMPORTANCE

This research will help traditional Dimasa Kacharis to be aware of the effectiveness of sacrifices. It will also educate them to resort to modern medical treatment rather than depending on expensive and elaborate sacrifices with the purpose of getting physical healing.

---

[5] K. K. Chatry, "Significance of Agricultural Festivals of Dimasa Kacharis in Assam" (M. Th. Thesis, Senate of Serampore College, 1998). Hereafter cited as Chatry, *Significance...*

[6] As per 2011 census, released by Directorate of Census Operations in Assam, out of the total population of Dima Hasao, 71.33% lives in rural areas of villages. "Dima Hasao District: Census 2011 data," http://www.census2011.co.in/census/district/150-dima-hasao.html (16 October 2012).

[7] T. Vanlatlani, *A Study of Religious Identity among the Bru of Mizoram* (Delhi: ISPCK, 2007), 36.

Moreover, this research may also have important contribution towards a better understanding and comprehension about the traditional Dimasa Kachari religion which survives lively against the influences of other religious faiths in their surroundings.

Furthermore, this research will hopefully be a valuable document on the traditional religion of the Dimasa Kacharis. It will also be an important resource for future researchers on the same line of this study.

The present work may also have valuable missiological implications by unearthing challenges for the Church in the on-going mission work among the Dimasa Kacharis.

4. SCOPE AND LIMITATION

In the midst of several religious elements, the traditional Dimasa Kachari practice of sacrifices is given focus because it has made several impacts upon their socio-economic and religious life. The geographical area of the research is limited to the Dima Hasao district in Assam.[8] In addition, another limitation which arises is hermeneutical suspicion causing unintended and unconscious prejudice, since the researcher is not a member of the Dimasa Kachari community. But this human tendency and weakness is kept within control as far as practicable.

5. PREVIOUS RESEARCH

Some scholars have done research on the Dimasa Kacharis. K.K. Chatry wrote, "Significance of Agricultural Festivals of Dimasa Kacharis in Assam" for his M. Th. Thesis in 1998 from Serampore College. Babul, Roy wrote "Socio-Cultural and Environmental Dimensions of Tribal Health: A Study among the Dimasa Kacharis and the Zeme Nagas of N. C. Hills in Assam" for his Ph. D. Thesis in 1998 from Gauhati University, Assam. But these scholars did not deal with the sacrifices of the traditional Dimasa Kacharis in detail. This

---

[8] As per 2001 census, the Dimasa Kachari population in Dima Hasao district was 64,881 while the total population was 128,428. "Basic Data Sheet District North Cachar Hills (20), Assam (18)," *Government of India Census 2001,* http://www.censusindia.gov.in/Tables_Published/Basic_Data_Sheet.aspx (16 October 2012).

research differs from the said researches as it is not a straightforward study or description of the various sacrifices, rather it goes further to make an earnest attempt in analyzing the sacrifices and their impact upon the socio-economic and religious life of the traditional Dimasa Kacharis. It also helps to find out the ways for making inter religious communication and dialogue easier at local levels.

6. METHODOLOGY IMPLEMENTED

To make a research comprehensive and reliable, the study of primal religions necessitates the employment of more than one methodology. Since religion of the traditional Dimasa Kacharis is a primal religion with no scriptural text, or systematic religious organization nor adequate documented sources to be employed, this research necessitates an application of the Anthropological Method which has proved to be the effective method for the study of primal religions. The Anthropological Method is the study of human beings, particularly the study of human culture in which religion is an integral part of culture; it also deals with people's language, customs and social institutions etc.[9]

Moreover, due to the nature of the research, the Sociological Approach is also engaged because it gives importance to human society and social facts by stressing that religion serves as a uniting factor of the human community. In this connection, Emile Durkheim's hypothesis that religion is 'society' and that religion unites human beings into 'one single moral community' is employed.[10]

Furthermore, Sociological Method investigates the inter-relatedness between society and religion. One of the chief concerns of Sociological Approach is to assess the impact of religiosity on individuals and society.[11] Accordingly, the researcher applies the

---

[9] Eric J. Lott, "Approaching a Religious Tradition," in *Religious Traditions of India*, edited by P.S. Daniel, David C. Scott and G. R. Singh (Delhi: ISPCK, 2002), 16.

[10] See K.P. Aleaz, *Dimensions of Indian Religion: Study, Experience and Interaction* (Calcutta: Punthi Pustak, 1995); Louis Schneider, *Sociological Approach to Religion* (New York: John Wiley & Sons Inc., 1970).

[11] S. Robertson, *Approaching Religion in a Pluralistic Context* (Bangalore: BTESSC/SATHRI, 2010), 27.

Sociological Method of study to assert the religion of the Dimasa Kacharis as a uniting factor which binds together the whole community into a single moral community, and that religion, in this case, the offering of sacrifices has certain negative as well as positive impacts upon the practicing community. Therefore, applying both Anthropological and Sociological Methods is preferable rather than applying only one method.

During this research both descriptive and analytical methods are applied as much as possible. Under descriptive method library resources like published and unpublished manuscripts, journals, magazines that are available are used. Under analytical method, two types of questionnaires were distributed: one type of questionnaire to traditional Dimasa Kacharis and the other to Christian Dimasa Kacharis. There are 70 traditional Dimasa Kacharis who responded and 18 Christian Dimasa Kacharis who responded (See the copy of the questionnaires in Appendix One and Two). Personal interviews with 13 persons were conducted to collect first-hand information about Dimasa Kachari sacrifices.

Chapter 2

SOCIO-ECONOMIC AND RELIGIOUS LIFE OF THE DIMASA KACHARIS

1. INTRODUCTION

In order to understand the issues that are to be dealt with in the course of this research, it is imperative that a chapter is dedicated to the people themselves. Therefore, this chapter gives a brief historical and etymological overview of the Dimasa Kacharis and an account of their socio-cultural institutions, religious beliefs and practices and their economic life. However, this chapter is not an attempt to be a detailed study of the history of the Dimasa Kacharis, therefore, only those elements that are important for the research are discussed in this chapter.

2. THE DIMASA KACHARIS

The Dimasa Kacharis belong to the great Bodo group of people and are the major ethnic group of the Dima Hasao District of Assam.[12] Linguistically the Dimasa Kacharis belong to the Tibeto-Burman group. The Dimasa Kacharis, the Boro-Kacharis and other

[12] G.C. Sarma Thakur, "Religious Beliefs and Folk Deities of the Dimasa Kacharis and Karbis of Assam," in *Selected Essays on Tribes and Castes of Assam Part-1,* G.C. Sarma Thakur (Guwahati: Directorate of Assam Institute of Research for

Kachari groups, like Koches, the Rabhas, the Lalungs, the Tipperas and others of North-East India refer to the same stock of people. However, there is among them much dissimilarity in matters of language and custom.[13] With regards to the etymological meaning of the term "Dimasa Kachari", there are diverse opinions among scholars. However, in the Dimasa Kachari dialect, the word "*Di*" means water, "*ma*" means great or big and "*sa*" means children. Hence, it is commonly accepted that *Dimasa* means "children of the great river."[14] Conversely, Hagzer is of the opinion that "Dimasa Kachari" is derived from *Dimapur sa,* i.e., the people who lived in Dimapur.[15]

Due to the absence of written documents, the early history of the Dimasa Kacharis can be regarded as a matter of surmise. However, their old legends point to the fact that after entering Assam they settled in the hills and slopes of the upper course of the Brahmaputra. They gradually moved westward and extended their settlement through central Assam to the Mymensing district of present Bangladesh.[16]

The Dimasa Kacharis first established their kingdom at Kamrupa and then at Sadiya. Thereafter they shifted their capital

---

Tribals and Scheduled Castes, 2007), 220. Hereafter cited as Thakur, *Religious beliefs...*

[13] The original home of the people belonging to the Tibeto-Burman race was in Western China near the Yang-Tze-Kiang and Hwang-ho rivers from where large numbers went down the courses of the Chinduwin and the Irrawady and then the Brahmaputra and started settling down in the valleys of these rivers and also in the remote hills adjacent to these valleys. See B.N. Bordoloi, G.C. Sarma Thakur and M.C. Saikia, *Tribes of Assam Part I* (Guwahati: Tribal Research Institute, 1987), 40. Hereafter cited as Bordoloi, Thakur and Saikia, *Tribes...*

[14] See Dinesh Tiwari and Gautam Sarma, "A historical and etymological study of the Dimasa Kacharis of Dima Hasao District, Assam, India," *The Clarion* 2/2 (2013); Ramdina Lalsim, *Tribes of N.C. Hills, Assam* (Haflong: Cultural & Publicity Officer, N.C. Hills Autonomous Council, Haflong, Assam, 2005). Hereafter cited as Lalsim, *Tribes...;* Sidney Endle, *The Kacharis* (Delhi: Cosmo Publications, 1975). Hereafter cited as Endle, *The Kacharis...*

[15] Nirupama Hagzer, *Dimasa* (Jorhat: Asom Sahitya Sabha, 1974), 1. Hereafter cited as Hagzer, *Dimasa...*

[16] Bordoloi, Thakur and Saikia, *Tribes...*, 41.

first to Dimapur and finally the Ahom king drove the people and their capital to Maibang in Dima Hasao by 1536 C.E. Again around 1750 C.E. they shifted their capital from Maibang to Khaspur in Cachar to escape from the frequent attacks of the Ahoms and the Jaintias.[17] Dimasa Kacharis now live mainly in Dima Hasao, Barak Valley, Sibsagar, Karbi Anglong and Nagaon districts of Assam.[18] A sizeable population is also found in Dimapur region of Nagaland.[19]

3. TERMINOLOGY AND ORIGIN OF THE TERM 'SACRIFICE' IN TRADITIONAL DIMASA KACHARI RELIGION

In the Dimasa Kachari language sacrifice is called '*bandai*'. The term is used with special reference to the sacrifice of blood offered to deities and spirits. It conveys the implication of a gift or an offering of thanksgiving or propitiation. Since sacrifice occupies a significant place in the Dimasa Kachari religion, it is necessary to trace the origin of sacrifice through one of their myths which goes like this.[20]

The creation narrative of the Dimasa Kacharis described in detail in section 6 (i) of this chapter speaks of the divine beings *Bangla Raja* and *Arikhidima* who were husband and wife. *Arikhidima* who is believed to be a big bird laid seven eggs and out of these six hatched naturally and six benevolent deities were born. When the seventh egg did not break in the course of time, the youngest and most mischievous deity *Hammiyadao* broke the egg by hitting it with a staff. Out of this seventh egg came many ugly and evil spirits who threatened to devour the whole world. In order to pacify them, *Bangla Raja* and *Arikhidima* decreed that henceforth these spirits would demand sacrifices of livestock from human beings

[17] S. Sengupta, "Kachari Dimasa," in *People of Assam Volume XV Part One*, edited by K.S. Singh (Calcutta: Anthropological Survey of India, 2003), 330. Hereafter cited as Sengupta, *Kachari Dimasa...*

[18] Kamal Narayan Choudhury, *Folklore in North-Eastern India* (Calcutta: Punthi Pustak, 2001), 217. Hereafter cited as Choudhury, *Folklore...*

[19] "Dimasa Kachari people," http://en.wikipedia.org/wiki/Dimasa Kachari_ people (2 July 2013). Hereafter cited as *Dimasa Kachari people...*

[20] Interview with Denon Naiding, resident of N.D. Razi, Haflong, 26 May 2013. Hereafter cited as Denon Naiding, Interview...

as propitiation. From that time onwards human beings have been offering sacrifices to appease the various evil spirits.

Although there are various versions, the creation narrative shows that sacrifice in the traditional Dimasa Kachari religion evolved out of fear and dread and in order to appease and propitiate the malevolent spirits that emerged from the seventh egg and who are believed to inhabit the physical environment surrounding the people. Moreover, sacrifice in the traditional Dimasa Kachari religion was a means of thanksgiving offered to divine and to receive blessings from it and thereby build a kind of bond between human and divine. However, it seems that the original motive of the sacrificers was to gratify the deity and strengthen their position in the deity's favour and maintain right relations between the community and the deity and thereby receive material blessings.

Thus, one can say that, sacrifice for the traditional Dimasa Kacharis, in the words of V.S. Lalrinawma, was a business transaction of "*do ut des*" (I give so that you will give in return) an activity without moral significance and it can be assumed that its purpose was to build relationship with the divine.[21]

4. SOCIO-CULTURAL FOUNDATIONS

The Dimasa Kacharis of Dima Hasao are interesting from the point of view of their differences with their kinspeople in the plains.[22] The distinctive socio-cultural foundations of the Dimasa Kacharis of Dima Hasao are as follows:

---

[21] V.S. Lalrinawma, *Mizo Ethos: Changes and Challenges* (Aizawl: Mizoram Publication Board, 2005), 102.

[22] While the latter have become completely assimilated with the Assamese or Bengalis in the Cachar plains, Barkataki asserts that the traditional Dimasa Kacharis of Dima Hasao have still preserved themselves to a certain extent as a tribal community with distinctive features. See S. Barkataki, *Tribes of Assam* (New Delhi: National Book Trust, India, 1984), 57.

i) Clan System

The most striking characteristic of the Dimasa Kachari social life is the existence of both male and female clans.[23] In order to trace their descent, the Dimasa Kachari primarily go by sex, i.e., a man traces his descent first through his paternal grandfather and secondly from the maternal grandmother whereas, a woman primarily traces her descent through her maternal grandmother and then secondly from her paternal grandfather. Thus, a Dimasa Kachari always bears allegiance to two clans. In the case of a man, his primary affiliation is with the father's patriclan (*Sengphong*) while his secondary affiliation is with the mother's matriclan (*Julu/Jaddi*).[24]

It should be mentioned that, in the case of a woman, her secondary affiliation, i.e., towards her paternal grandfather changes to her husband's *Sengphong* as soon as she gets married. But her primary affiliation with the *Jaddi* remains unchanged.[25] Therefore, one can say that the Dimasa Kachari society is a patrilineal as well as matrilineal society.

Clan exogamy is the general rule, and as far as the rule of marriage is concerned, a man cannot marry a girl of his father's *Sengphong* and mother's *Jaddi*. A girl also cannot marry a man whose mother belongs to her *Jaddi* and who belongs to her father's *Sengphong*. If any person violates the clan exogamy, he/she is instantly excommunicated from the society. No one is allowed to marry within his/her own clan.[26] S.T. Das also observes that, marriage within one's *Sengphong* or *Jaddi* is not permissible and they strictly follow the rules laid down by

---

[23] There are 40 male clans (*Sengphong*) and 42 female clans (*Julu* or *Jaddi*). Both the male and female clans are exogamous and no marriage can take place between boys and girls of the same clan. See S.K. Barpujari, *History of the Dimasa: From the Earliest Times to 1896 A.D.* (Haflong: R. Langthasa, Cultural and Publicity Officer, Autonomous Council, N.C. Hills (Assam), Haflong, 1997), 122. Hereafter cited as Barpujari, *History...*

[24] Dipali G. Danda, *Among the Dimasa of Assam: An Ethnographic Study* (New Delhi: Sterling Publishers Pvt. Ltd., 1978), 42. Hereafter cited as Danda, *Among the Dimasa...*

[25] Danda, *Among the Dimasa...*, 43.

[26] Danda, *Among the Dimasa...*, 45.

their traditional customs.[27] Here mention may be made of the fact that a woman automatically loses her *Sengphong* on marriage and joins her husband's *Sengphong* with the solemnization of a ceremony *madaikhilimba*,[28] but her *Jaddi* remains unchanged. The only relation that remains with her father's *Sengphong* is that if she ever remarries, she must avoid selecting someone belonging to her father's *Sengphong*. In the case of a divorce, a woman automatically loses her husband's *Sengphong* and bears her original affiliation.[29]

The clan system is so rigid that every member must fulfill all the clan obligations. If the members of the *Sengphong* and *Jaddi* are not invited to the funeral feast of a person, it is considered to be a serious transgression. C. A. Soppit also affirms the importance of their clan system and its implication by saying; "All Kacharis are clannish, and an insult or offence to any one of them being often taken up by the whole village or community."[30]

ii) Marriage

In matters related to marriage also, the clan is the major institution which regulates marriage. Marriage is strictly a monogamous institution and child marriage is not practiced in the Dimasa Kachari society. Widow re-marriage is allowed; a younger brother may marry his elder brother's widow, but an elder brother cannot marry his younger brother's widow. In the same way, a man can marry the younger sister of his wife but not her elder sister. Cross-cousin marriage is permitted provided the rules of clan exogamy are not violated.[31]

---

[27] S. T. Das, *Life Style: Indian Tribes: Locational Practice, Vol. I* (Delhi: Gyan Publishing House, 1987), 97. Hereafter cited as Das, *Life Style...*

[28] *Madaikhilimba* means the worship of clan deities. It must be performed within one week from marriage by the groom's father. It is dealt in detail in Chapter Three Section 3 (ii)

[29] Das, *Life Style...*, 46.

[30] C. A. Soppit, *Historical and Descriptive Account of Kachari Tribes in N.C. Hills with Specimen of Tales and Folklore* (Shillong: The Assam Secretariat Press, 1885), 13.

[31] B.N. Bordoloi, *The Dimasa Kacharis of Assam* (Guwahati: Tribal Research Institute, 1984), 54. Hereafter cited as Bordoloi, *The Dimasa Kacharis...*

Marriage is usually through negotiation, even though the consent of the boy and girl is also taken into consideration. In the case of such negotiated marriages, the father and elder male relative of the boy visits the girl's house on a fixed date and start negotiations. After two more such visits from the boy's side the date for the marriage is fixed. In course of the final negotiation, the bride-price known as *kalti*[32] is also settled. Besides this expenditure, the groom has to offer all expenses for the feast to be held at the bride's place.[33] Among the Christian Dimasa Kacharis of Dima Hasao, the *kalti* has been fixed at Rs. 505.[34]

A marriage arranged by parents through negotiation is called *disingba*, while marriage by mutual consent which is known as *khaolaba*, elopement and intrusion is not totally absent among the Dimasa Kacharis.[35] Just before leaving for the bride's village the boy's father performs *Mayofagarba* which means the worshipping of all deities.[36] On entering into the bride's village, a pig which is carried with the bridegroom's party is sacrificed by the boy's father for a blessed marital life. This ritual is called *midogarba*.[37]

iii) Festivals[38]

The Dimasa Kacharis of Dima Hasao, being agrarian people, celebrate various agricultural festivals in different ways on different occasions.

---

[32] The amount of *kalti* varies from Rs. 30 – Rs. 500 depending upon the economic capacity of the bridegroom as well as the "quality" of the bride.

[33] Barpujari, *History*..., 126.

[34] Interview with Mr. Phonendra Naiding, a Christian Dimasa Kachari living in Haflong, 18 November 2013. Hereafter cited as Phonendra Naiding, Interview...

[35] Singh, *People*..., 331.

[36] Hagzer, *Dimasa*..., 28.

[37] The various sacrifices connected with marriage will be dealt in detail in Chapter Three Section 3 (ii).

[38] Festivals for the tribals symbolize 're-dedication of life'. In these festivals, many religious ceremonies are involved. Therefore, these festivals, for the tribals are not only occasions for eating, drinking and merry making. In fact, these festivals have deep religious significances for them. These festivals also present the tribals with the opportunity to worship together as a community, thus providing social cohesion and unity to the various members of the community. The Dimasa Kachari traditional festivals are also a combination of socio-economic and religious elements

These festivals can be classified into festivals involving the entire Dimasa Kachari community and festivals observed by each village. The local festivals are performed by each village separately, and participation is also restricted to the people of the concerned village.[39]

These festivals whose celebrations contain a lot of sacrificial rituals and elements are *Krongfanggarba*[40] and *Maisalaigarba,*[41] *Misengba*[42] and *Busu.*[43] The celebration of these festivals plays an important role in the preservation of the traditional beliefs and practices, and they will be described elaborately in Chapter Three.

5. ECONOMIC LIFE

The Dimasa Kacharis are economically backward due to various factors such as the remoteness of their habitats from the state capital and the absence of a permanent source of cash income among them. In fact, in 2006 the Indian government named Dima Hasao one of the country's 250 most backward districts (out of a total of 640).[44]

---

and would be incomplete without the offering of sacrifices. Hence, J. Troisi has defined 'festival' as a wider term referring to a community celebration which usually combines social, economic and religious elements. See J. Troisi, *Tribal Religion: Religious Beliefs and Practices among the Santals* (New Delhi: Manohar Publishers and Distributors, 1979), 115.

[39] Zahid Ahmed Tapadar, comp., *Festivals of N.C. Hills* (Haflong: Department of Information and Public Relations, N.C. Hills, Haflong, Assam, 2007-2008), 15. Hereafter cited as Tapadar, comp., *Festivals…*

[40] *Krongfanggarba* is an annual agricultural sacrifice performed for the welfare and protection of a village and for good harvest. It is described in detail in Chapter Three Section 2 (ii).

[41] *Maisalaigarba* is an annual agricultural sacrifice performed for community welfare and good harvest. It is described in detail in Chapter Three Section 2 (iii).

[42] *Misengba* is a community sacrifice involving the entire Dimasa Kachari community. It is offered for the purification of the land and the people and for communal harmony. It is described in detail in Chapter Three Section 2 (i).

[43] *Busu* is not actually a sacrifice. It is an annual harvest festival but it has religious implications and sacrifices occupy an integral position in the celebration. It is described in detail in Chapter Three Section 2 (v).

[44] According to the District Rural Development Agency (DRDA), Dima Hasao, there are 30,919 families with BPL Cards. District Rural Development Agency, Dima Hasao, Assam, *Statistical Report for the year 2012*, 2012.

It is one of the eleven districts in Assam currently receiving funds from the Backward Regions Grant Fund Programme (BRGF).[45] Although there are other economic sources, the main occupation of the Dimasa Kachari is shifting cultivation (*jhum*) and the land is the main economic resource.

i) Agriculture

Agriculture is the principal occupation and the main source of livelihood for the Dimasa Kacharis. They practice shifting cultivation though they also have permanent wet cultivation fields wherever possible.

Their main agricultural items are rice, *Maizu* (special rice for tiffin and ricebeer), brinjal, white pumpkin, red pumpkin, chilli, cotton, etc. Besides these, bananas, papayas and oranges are also being introduced in some Dimasa Kachari villages.[46] For the protection of crops and a good harvest, they observe several pre and post-cultivation ceremonies which will be discussed in Chapter Three.

ii) Livestock

In the socio-economic life, domesticated animals and birds are required not only for domestic consumption and commercial purposes, but also for the performance of sacrificial rites and rituals and during the celebration of the festivals.

The main livestock reared by the Dimasa Kacharis are fowls, pigs, goats, ducks and buffaloes. The Dimasa Kacharis highly value buffalo meat[47] and this particular animal is being reared till today by the villagers. Besides these, dogs and cats are also domesticated but their meats are not eaten.

---

[45] "Dima Hasao district," http://familypedia.wikia.com/wiki/Dima_Hasao_district (2 July 2013).

[46] Lalsim, *Tribes…*, 6.

[47] The buffalo is highly valued and the person possessing a large number of buffaloes is considered to be a wealthy person; such person is accorded high social status and dignity. Moreover, in community sacrifices involving the entire Dimasa Kachari community, many buffaloes are sacrificed and this particular animal constitutes one of the most sacrificed animals.

iii) Cottage Industry

Weaving and spinning occupies a major cottage industry of the Dimasa Kachari women. Every Dimasa Kachari woman has her own traditional pit loom and the art of weaving is of special interest and importance to every Dimasa Kachari woman who has to start learning the art from a very early age.[48] So important is the art of weaving for the women that Chatry states, "it is a must for young girls to learn weaving clothes and cooking food. If a girl does not know weaving she may not get a husband."[49]

Besides the textile technology, Dimasa Kachari artisans are experts in cane and bamboo works. They manufacture different types of bamboo mats, baskets both artistic and ordinary, fishing traps and other household equipment. Some bamboo mats used for special occasions are very artistically designed with colours.[50] During the offering of sacrifices, bamboo baskets known as *longkhai,*[51] cups and plates made of bamboo and small clay figurines depicting humans, buffaloes, deers, etc., are also utilized in multiple ways.

6. TRADITIONAL RELIGIOUS BELIEFS AND CONCEPTS

The Dimasa Kacharis have their own traditional religious heritage which is orally transmitted from foreparents to present day generation. In spite of the influence of Hinduism, Christianity and other religious faiths, Chatry affirms that, the credit goes to the traditional Dimasa Kacharis, of rural areas in Dima Hasao, for preserving their valuable ancient religious heritages.[52] Endle and others consider the religion of the Kacharis as definitely of the type usually known as 'animistic' and its basic principle is typically one of fear and dread.

---

[48] Lalsim, *Tribes...*, 10.

[49] Chatry, *Significance...*

[50] G.K. Ghosh, *Tribals and their Culture in Assam, Meghalaya and Mizoram, Vol. 1* (New Delhi: Ashish Publishing House, 1992), 23. Hereafter cited as Ghosh, *Tribals...*

[51] It is a basket made of bamboo and used for carrying paddy.

[52] K.K. Chatry, "Ecological Significance of the Traditional Beliefs and Practices of Dimasa Kachari Tribe, *Indian Journal of Theology 43/1&2* (2001), 64.

Although elements of animism are found in the traditional Dimasa Kachari religion, the term 'animism' is not sufficient for defining it because Dimasa Kachari religion contains much more than what has been meant by 'animism'.[53] Hence, Longchar has also contended, "…to look at a religion in that way (animistic way) is quite dehumanizing and irrational."[54]

i) Creation Narrative

According to the Dimasa Kachari creation narrative, in the beginning the world was completely uninhabited and the shape of the rivers, mountains, trees and plants, etc., were not the same as it is today. An unearthly silence had enveloped the whole atmosphere. In course of time two divine beings one male and one female appeared and their appearance broke the unearthly and all-pervading silence of the earth. The male was called *Bangla Raja* and the female was called *Arikhidima*. *Bangla Raja* is considered to be the deity of earthquake while *Arikhidima* is believed to be a big bird.[55]

Bangla Raja and his consort *Arikhidima* lived in a place called *Damra*. *Arikhidima* who had a divine conception could not find a suitable place to lay her eggs. A Golden Eagle was sent to search a suitable place in the confluence of *Dilao* and *Sangi* rivers. There *Arikhidima* laid seven eggs, out of which she successfully hatched six benevolent deities. The seventh egg which did not break in the

---

[53] Animism is the belief in spiritual beings getting involved with human affairs and capable of helping or harming humans. The Dimasa Kachari religion, like other primal religions, undoubtedly contains some elements of 'animism'. However, the animistic belief is only one of the elements. The Dimasa Kacharis, like other primal people, believe in taboo, omen, witchcraft, magic and other elements which are the distinctive traits of the major religious traditions. The Dimasa Kacharis revere nature because it is believed to be inhabited by deities and spirits. Nature reminds the Dimasa Kacharis of the creative power of the Supreme god. These various elements form the core of human existence, and are pertinent even today. So, it would be unreasonable to simply categorize the traditional Dimasa Kachari religion as 'animistic.'

[54] A. Wati Longchar, *The Tribal Religious Traditions in North East India – An Introduction* (Jorhat: Eastern Theological College, 1991), 6. Hereafter cited as Longchar, *Tribal Religious Traditions…*

[55] Ghosh, *Tribals…*, 21-22.

natural course when broken produced ugly shaped evil spirits causing wide spread chaos. The Dimasa Kacharis consider themselves to be the descendants of the above mentioned six benevolent deities, whereas the evil spirits which came out of the seventh egg dwell in the hills and rivers are considered responsible for causing diseases, calamities and sufferings and are to be appropriately worshipped.[56]

ii) Concept of Supreme God (*Madai*)

Although they believe in the existence of a Supreme god, the traditional Dimasa Kachari concept of Supreme god is very ambiguous. However, they believe that there is an All Creator living in the heaven. Since he is considered to be harmless, their attitude toward him is rather indifferent. This Supreme god is called *Madai*.[57] They do not seem to have any prescribed form of worship for the Supreme god.[58]

Even though the Dimasa Kachari concept of Supreme god is very vague, one can comprehend that the Supreme god is above all other deities and spirits. The other deities including the ancestral deities are created beings, born of the seven eggs of *Bangla Raja* and *Arikhidima* and confined to specific areas. However, *Madai*, the

---

[56] There are several versions of this creation narrative. This particular version is the one narrated by S.K. Barpujari. Another version narrated by K.K. Chatry goes like this: In the process of time one of the eggs broke and was born *Sibrai*. When he came out of the egg he saw nothing, then, he created the heaven and the earth, and all kinds of trees, plants and living things. After he finished the work of creation he again went inside the egg. Subsequently other eggs started breaking and were born *Du Raja*, *Naiku Raja*, *Wa Raja*, *Bongyung-Faiyung* and *Hammiyadao* from the second, third, fourth, fifth and sixth eggs respectively. The seventh egg did not break for a long time and caused worry among the brothers. The egg was called *Balamba*, meaning spoiled one. *Hammiyadao*, the youngest brother, was a naughty one who hit the egg very hard with a staff and broke it. Immediately after the egg was broken there came out many ugly shaped and evil spirits and threatened to devour the whole world, causing widespread chaos. At last *Sibrai*, the eldest brother pacified the spirits by ordaining their habitats and living. See Barpujari, ed., *History*...; Chatry, *Significance*...

[57] Danda, *Among the Dimasa*..., 131.

[58] Ghosh, *Tribals*..., 25.

Supreme god is Omnipresent, Creator, Eternal and self-existent and even his dwelling place is unknown to the people.

Hence, although there is no prescribed form of worship for the Supreme god, till today the blessings of the Supreme god is sought and prayers are offered to him on any auspicious occasion such as marriage, harvest-festival, etc., with folded hands "*Madai jingkhe hamthai rinang*," which means, "May god bless us."[59]

iii) Area Deity and Clan Deity

The six deities that were produced by the 6 eggs of *Arikhidima* are considered to be the ancestral deities by the Dimasa Kacharis and the entire Dimasa Kachari land is believed to be under their jurisdiction.

In olden times the whole Dimasa Kachari land was divided into twelve religious *daikhos*.[60] The people believed that deities resided in a particular *daikho* and that they protected the people of that area and controlled their destiny. The deities of different *daikhos* do not possess representative images and at the time of worship are usually symbolized by raising earthen mounds. They are worshipped along with their spouses and children for whom also similar mounds are raised.[61]

Danda believes that from this concept of area deity the concept of clan deity has evolved.[62] The Dimasa Kacharis who possess great loyalty to their respective clans have the tradition of worshipping the clan deities by offering sacrifice known as *Sengphong Nimadai* which will be discussed in Chapter Three Section 2 (iv).

iv) Deities and Spirits

The Dimasa Kacharis also strongly believe in the existence of various deities and spirits who are scattered around their physical environment and who get involved in their day to day life. In fact, it is these deities

---

[59] Phonendra Naiding, Interview…

[60] *Daikhos* are the abodes or unstructured shrines of the area deities. The twelve religious *daikhos* are as follows: i) *Alu*, ii) *Baigiai*, iii) *Hamri*, iv) *Daman*, v) *Longmailai*, vi) *Manja*, vii) *Misim*, viii) *Mongrang*, ix) *Ranchandi*, x) *Riao*, xi) *Waibra* and xii) *Woa*. See Bordoloi, *The Dimasa Kacharis…*, 72.

[61] Barpujari, ed., *History…*, 141.

[62] Danda, *Among the Dimasa…*, 127.

and spirits who play a pivotal role in the traditional Dimasa Kachari religion. In order to avoid their wrath and to co-exist with them peacefully, they are propitiated and appeased by offering sacrifices and prayers on numerous occasions.[63] The deities are believed to be benevolent and are propitiated for the general welfare of the family and the village. They are considered to be harmless even if they are not worshipped annually.

On the other hand, the spirits are believed to be malevolent and having control over human beings in some way or the other. If they are not propitiated properly, they are believed to inflict sufferings upon the people. Therefore, the Dimasa Kacharis are more careful to observe sacrifices offered to the malevolent spirits.

Therefore, one can assume that there is a definite hierarchy in the Dimasa Kachari pantheon. First, there is the Supreme god, who is self-existent and Creator of all. Second, there is the original divine couple *Bangla Raja* and *Arikhidima*. Then comes the six ancestral deities born of the six eggs laid by *Arikhidima*. They are followed by minor deities who are considered to be benevolent. Lastly, there are the malevolent spirits born of the seventh egg of *Arikhidima*. Hence, in the course of this research, the term 'god' is used to refer solely to the Supreme god while the term 'deity' is used to refer to the benevolent deities and six ancestral deities. The term 'spirit' is used to denote the malevolent spirits.

v) Concept of Life after Death

The traditional Dimasa Kacharis believe in reincarnation of the soul. It is believed that the body is subject to death and decay, but the soul never dies.[64] According to the Dimasa Kachari belief, after death human beings go to *Damra* which is equivalent to heaven.[65] *Damra* is the ancestor's spirit world where the dead ones go before they take

---

[63] Besides the six ancestral deities, some of the other deities of the Dimasa Kacharis are *Ranchandi*, *Hedemdi*, *Dilauju*, *Dinkau*, *Dichaim*, *Kachaim*, *Cham Biyam* and *Larikangang*. See Hagzer, *Dimasa...*, 75.

[64] Hagzer, *Dimasa*, 61.

[65] Barpujari, ed., *History...*, 143.

rebirth. It is the land of the dead.[66] It is believed that in *Damra,* the dead retain their earthly nature and longings.

The traditional Dimasa Kacharis believe that, one's condition in the next birth depends upon one's earthly deeds. In order to have a birth in human form, a person has to perform all duties towards the family and the village properly. In other words, in order to be reborn as a human being, a person must lead an honest life and follow the established rules and norms of the society. A person who violates the norms of society may be reincarnated as an animal or he/she may not be reincarnated at all, but be left to wander in the air like a spirit which for the Dimasa Kachari is a severe punishment upon the human soul. Danda emphatically states that in the traditional Dimasa Kachari theology, there is no concept of salvation of the soul.[67]

The concept of life and death makes the people cautious in performing the funeral ceremony and the ceremonial offerings of food and drink, because it is believed that if these are not correctly done, the spirit of the deceased person does not find a place in the other world and will wander with great wretchedness in the locality of the village.[68]

vi) Observance of Taboo

Taboo is a Polynesian word which means "prohibited" or "forbidden".[69] For Presler, "...*taboo* indicates those caution established to guard against supernaturally dangerous things, plants, animals or persons, specifically those possessing *mana*."[70] Taboo extends to actions also. Hence, any action that violates the community norm brings the supernatural penalty. Thus, Kechutzer says that, taboo is a sacred

---

[66] Chatry, *Significance...*

[67] Danda, *Among the Dimasa...*, 131.

[68] Hagzer, *Dimasa*, 61.

[69] Ninian Smart, *The Religious Experience of Mankind*, 3rd ed. (New York: Charles Scribner & Sons, 1984), 34-35.

[70] H. H. Presler, *Primitive Religion in India* (Madras: CLS, 1971), 10. Hereafter cited as Presler, *Primitive Religion...*

interdict that takes into account the power that surrounds certain objects and activities.[71]

In the traditional Dimasa Kachari society, it is taboo to cut certain trees as it is considered to be inhabited by spirits; disregarding this taboo could result in divine punishment of the person and his/her clan. It is also taboo to cultivate the land in which those trees are found. If anyone wants to cultivate in such plot, *Majhai Khilingba* which is dealt in detail in Chapter Three Section 3 (iv), must be performed before the land is cultivated. Moreover, they do not cultivate such land where there are huge trees, rocks, sources of springs and ponds.

These taboos seem to be related to the concept of *daikhoism* as they believe that area-deities are considered to have their abodes in different forest patches. The deities residing in a particular *daikho* protect the people of that area and control their destiny. These *daikhos* are very important and these forest patches are conserved till today through the community participation.[72]

All these observance of taboos related to the land shows the belief that the whole creation belongs to *Madai*. For the traditional Dimasa Kacharis, the trees and plants are not simply inanimate objects, but are thriving and belong to the Supreme god. Such kind of injunctions helps preservation of the natural resources. In the traditional Dimasa Kachari religion, taboo is also observed in every religious act. The festival days are religious Holy-days when no work is to be done by the whole community. The whole community and creation takes rest to worship the deities and to rejoice.

The traditional Dimasa Kacharis rear buffaloes, but it is taboo for them to consume or sell its milk as they believe that the young

---

[71] Sashikaba Kechutzar, "Rethinking Naga Religious Traditions: An Exploration of Tribal Christian Spirituality," in *Theologizing Tribal Heritage – A Critical Re-Look*, edited by Hrangthan Chhungi (Delhi: CWM/ISET-ECC/PCI/ISPCK, 2008), 175. Hereafter cited as Kechutzer, *Rethinking*…

[72] Pramod Medhi and Sachin Kumar Borthakur, "Sacred groves and sacred plants of the Dimasas of North Cachar Hills of Northeast India," *African Journal of Plant Science* 7/2, (February, 2013): 68.

ones should not be deprived of the mother's milk.[73] It is also taboo to rear or eat the flesh of cows as they are considered *gusu* (impure).[74]

The observance or non-observance of the various taboos affects not only the individual but the whole community and the creation. Many of these taboos may be revoked by the observance of sacrificial rituals which will be dealt with in Chapter Three.

vii) Religious Specialists and Functionaries

No female religious specialists or functionaries are found among the traditional Dimasa Kacharis. The various religious functionaries are as follows:

a) *Gisia*

The *Gisia* is the highest religious leader of the Dimasa Kacharis. The principal functions of the *Gisia* are the preparation of the holy water called *dithar*[75] and giving to the *Zonthais* before the celebration of *Misengba* festival. The *Gisia* ordains the *Zonthais* and his presence is central to the *Misengba* festival. In order to be a *Gisia*, one must abstain from eating pork, doing business or holding any kind of secular or civil office.[76] The *Gisia* is the most sacred and most respected among the Dimasa Kachari because he is holy and sacred and does not need to drink *dithar*.

b) *Zonthai*

A *Zonthai* is the religious functionary of a particular clan within a *daikho*. The main function of the *Zonthai* is overseeing and performing all necessary sacrificial rituals during *Misengba* under the authority of the *Gisia*. He also has to purify an impure person by

---

[73] Thakur, *Religious beliefs…*, 237.

[74] Many traditional Dimasa Kacharis believe that on becoming a Christian and at the time of receiving Baptism, one has to drink the urine of a cow. Moreover, they believe that since Christians eat cow's meat they are '*gusu*', i.e., impure. Interview with Joton Hojai, a Dimasa Christian and resident of Boildhura, Dima Hasao, 15 November 2013. Hereafter cited as Joton Hojai, Interview…

[75] *Dithar* is the holy water which the *Gisia* prepares by mixing the blood of the sacrificial animal with water.

[76] Chatry, *Significance…*

giving him/her *dithar* and worship the clan deity for the well-being of the clan living within the *daikho*. A *Zonthai* has to observe the above mentioned restrictions as well. There can be many *Zonthais* within a particular *daikho*.

c) ***Dainya and Baroa***

The main function of the *Dainya* is to sacrifice buffaloes during the celebration of the *Misengba* festival. The function of the *barao* is to hold the sacrificial animal at the time of sacrifice. He also offers sacrifices of smaller animals such as he-goats and fowls to the deities.[77] A *Baroa* is the helper of a *Zonthai* within a specific area.

d) ***Hojai***

Hojai is a religious specialist of a particular village. He performs death rituals and other ceremonies in the village. During the celebration of village festivals his service as a priest is required by the village people. Any person can become *Hojai* if he undergoes training for some time under a *Hojai*.[78]

But a person who has been bitten by a dog cannot become a *Hojai*.[79] There is no restriction for a *Hojai* concerning eating, drinking, shaving etc.

e) ***Phatri***

Phatri is a person through whom the deities convey their will to the people. He is not a formal religious specialist. It is not a hereditary office. Deities can possess any person whom they choose. However, Bordoloi is of the opinion that, *Phatris* are wise and well-versed in the performance of religious rites.[80] Since the Dimasa Kacharis believe

---

[77] Chatry, *Significance...*

[78] Interview with Sarda Hojai, former Hojai and resident of Natun Wari, Dima Hasao, 26 May 2013. Hereafter cited as Sarda Hojai, Interview...

[79] The reason why a person bitten by a dog cannot become a *Hojai* is that, in the traditional Dimasa Kachari religion, religious functionaries must be physically faultless. Moreover, dogs are considered unclean because of their scavenging habits. Hence, a person bitten by an unclean animal becomes faulty and unfit to render religious service. Sarda Hojai, Interview...

[80] Bordoloi, *The Dimasa Kacharis...*, 74.

that the monthly flow of blood renders a person impure, women cannot be *Phatris*.

f) Other Specialists and Functionaries

Other than the aforementioned religious functionaries, another functionary connected with the Dimasa Kachari religion is the *Gorashali*. A *Gorashali* is a person who can correctly identify the spirit causing sickness by using a bamboo, the entrails of a chicken, cowrie shells, bamboo sticks etc. The method of diagnosing needs to be learnt. The *Gorashali* is not a formal religious functionary and his sole function is to correctly identify the malevolent spirit causing the sickness. The required sacrifice to appease the spirit must be offered by the *Hojai*.[81] In lieu of his services the *Gorashali* does not demand any payment but the people are free to offer him in cash or kind as they deem fit.

The idea of witchcraft, although uncommon, is also prevalent among the Dimasa Kacharis. It is believed that some women have the power of committing evil through witchcraft. These women are called *Sagainjik* and people try to avoid them by all means. They are believed to cause harm even to unborn babies simply by gazing at pregnant women.[82]

7. CONCLUDING REMARKS

Therefore, one can see that the Dimasa Kacharis are a tribe with their own unique socio-cultural structure, economic system and religious beliefs and practices that are intertwined with one another.

Furthermore, the Dimasa Kachari traditional religion with its inestimable rites, rituals and sacrifices prove the assertion of Longchar that, tribal religion[83] is the innumerable rites

[81] Interview with Tarzen Langthasa, resident of N.D. Razi, Haflong, 26 May 2013. Hereafter cited as Tarzen Langthasa, Interview...

[82] Danda, *Among the Dimasa...*, 137.

[83] The terms 'tribe' and 'tribal' are commonly used to refer to the people who still practice their traditional beliefs. The Indian Constitution in spite of its extensive use of the term 'tribes' does not give any definition or explanation. However, 'tribe' or 'tribal' does not necessarily mean that these people are still living in primitive or backward stage of life. Hence, Wati Longchar has intensely argued that the term

and rituals that begin from the womb till death which leads to the afterlife.[84]

A unique characteristic of tribal religion is that, it does not have a written scripture like other religions. Their religious ethos is embodied in their myths, legends, folktales and stories.[85] Likewise, the traditional Dimasa Kachari religion has been preserved in the form of myths, rites and rituals that have been preserved and handed down orally from one generation to another.

Longchar further asserts that, in the tribal religion, an individual's life and the community life are inseparable.[86] Correspondingly for a Dimasa Kachari, to be truly human is to belong to the whole community, including the ancestors and creation. In order to do that, one must actively participate in the beliefs, ceremonies, rituals and festivals of the community.

Thus, one can conclude by saying that, the sacrificial rites and rituals are closely related to their socio-cultural and economic lives. These sacrificial rites and rituals have united the Dimasa Kacharis and given them their uniqueness and identity. They have helped them to preserve their age-old traditional beliefs and practices in the face of several influencing factors.

'tribal religion' does not refer to the backwardness of the practitioners. It rather refers to a living religion believed and practiced by many people of the world that is still vibrant, living and growing. Therefore, as stated by T. Vanlaltlani, tribal religion is "the basic of religious beliefs and practices of the people who were, once, called primitive, original, indigenous, and native in the past, and have been called developed or modern people in the changing years of age due to the change of the life of its practitioners. See Longchar, *Tribal Religious Traditions*...; T. Vanlaltlani, *Tribal Religion: Mizo and Bru* (Aizawl: Mizo Theological Association, 2009). [Hereafter cited as T. Vanlaltlani, *Tribal Religion*...

[84] A. Wati Longchar, *The Traditional Tribal Worldview and Modernity* (Jorhat: Eastern Theological College, 2000), 6.

[85] Yangkahao Vashum, "Sources for Developing Tribal Theology," in *An Exploration of Tribal Theology*, edited by Wati Longchar (Jorhat: The Tzudikong Baptist Church, 1997), 66.

[86] Longchar, *Tribal Religious Traditions*..., 3.

Chapter 3

SACRIFICES OF THE TRADITIONAL DIMASA KACHARIS

1. INTRODUCTION

As mentioned in Chapter One Section 2, the various sacrifices of the traditional Dimasa Kacharis of Dima Hasao district may be broadly classified into community sacrifices and individual sacrifices.

The traditional Dimasa Kacharis being agrarian occupants celebrate various festivals on the basis of changing agricultural seasons. In the celebration of their festivals, sacrifices occupy an integral part of the celebration process. Moreover, due to their belief in the existence of malevolent spirits as well as benevolent deities, every ailment is attributed to be the work of malevolent spirits. Hence, curative sacrifices occupy an important place in the life of every Dimasa Kachari.

Therefore, in this chapter, the various community as well as individual sacrifices of the traditional Dimasa Kacharis have been described in detail.

2. COMMUNITY SACRIFICES

Sacrifices concerning the entire Dimasa Kachari community are two in number, viz., *Misengba* and *Busu*. *Misengba* is a community sacrifice that is performed once in five or seven years and all the traditional Dimasa Kacharis, except women are obligated to participate both physically as well as through monetary contributions in the observance of this sacrifice. On the other hand, *Busu* is observed annually with much pomp and splendor.

i) *Misengba* (Sacrifice for Purification and Communal Harmony)

Misengba is a sacrifice in which the traditional Dimasa Kacharis worship and offer sacrifices to all the different clan and family deities simultaneously. In olden times, this sacrifice seems to have been performed annually. However, due to the huge expenses involved, the annual sacrifice was abandoned and today it is offered once in five or seven years.

a) Purpose

The performance of this sacrifice is meant for the purification of the land and the people from all kinds of impurities that leads to the suffering of the land and the people. Palon Ch. Warisa says that it is a must to perform *Misengba* at least once in seven years or else the people would be subject to immense troubles and hardships in the form of famines, diseases, widespread killing of people by tigers etc.[87]

K. Daulagupu says that *Misengba* is performed when there is widespread enmity among the different clans, communal disharmony, misfortunes and calamities. If all is well, then *Misengba* may not be performed. However, *Wadumaniba*, a lesser sacrifice, is offered in lieu of *Misengba* to show that the *Misengba* is observed.[88] Sajal Bathari is of the opinion that even though this sacrifice is performed by the Dimasa Kacharis only, it is meant for the welfare of all the various tribes including non-Dimasas also.[89]

[87] Interview with Palon Ch. Warisa, retired Govt. servant and resident of Sarkari Bagan, Haflong, 12 November 2013. Hereafter cited as Warisa, Interview…

[88] Interview with K. Daulagupu, Hojai and resident of Haflong, 19 November 2013. Hereafter cited as Daulagupu, Interview…

[89] Interview with Sajal Bathari, resident of N.D. Razi, Haflong, 20 November 2013. Hereafter cited as Sajal Bathari, Interview…

b) Preparations

The time for offering this sacrifice is determined by the *Phatri* through divination or oracles. Therefore, the time is divinely fixed and not by humans.[90] After the date of sacrifice has been announced, all the *Khunangs* (traditional headmen) of all the twelve *daikhos* meet together and constitute a celebration committee called *Misengba Melkhamba* to organize the sacrifice and to fix the amount to be contributed by each village. All the expenses for the sacrifice are borne willingly by the villagers as fixed by the *Misengba Melkhamba.*

Unlike other sacrifices, *Misengba* can be performed only in certain particular places called *Madaikhos;*[91] viz., *Abungbra, Dugubra* and *Mahurbra.* These three places are situated in the confluence of rivers. *Misengba* is performed in all three places at the same time. Among the three places, *Abungbra* is the most important; hence it requires the presence of the highest priest *Gisia.* Since, the *Gisia* cannot be present in all the three places at the same time, in the other two places, the *Zonthais* of the two *daikhos* oversee and performs their respective functions of executing all necessary sacrificial rituals under the authority of the *Gisia.*[92]

c) *Misengba* Sacrifice

The most auspicious day for the performance of the sacrifice is Sunday. Palon Ch. Warisa is of the view that the first sacrifice was probably performed on Sunday, and hence it continued to be performed on Sunday. Dark nights are regarded as the nights of evil spirits, but bright nights are believed to be the nights when blessings from the deities are received.[93]

---

[90] Sajal Bathari, Interview…

[91] According to Padmini Langthasa, *Madai* means invisible deities and *kho* means the home or place. Hence, *Madaikho* means the home of deities. See Padmini Langthasa, "Traditional Methods of Conflict Management among the Dimasa," in *Traditional Method of Conflict Resolution in Three Tribal Societies of North East India*, edited by Alphonsus D'Souza (Guwahati: North Eastern Social Research Centre, 2011), 14-15.

[92] Lalsim, *Tribes…*, 21-22.

[93] Warisa, Interview…

On this day, traditional male Dimasa Kacharis of all the twelve *daikhos* gather together at the three *Madaikhos* with all necessary materials. K. Daulagupu says that, the people who are offering the sacrifices must be purified with new clothes of white colour and no shoes must be worn in the sacrificial place in the jungle.[94] Women, children, the very old and weak and impure persons are not allowed to participate in the sacrifice and they remain in the villages.

On Saturday morning, the *Gisia* takes bath and prepares holy water called *dithar* and gives it to the *Zonthais,* and in turn *Zonthais* give holy water to the people. Thus, all priests and the people get purified for the celebration. However, the *Gisia* does not need to take *dithar* because he is holy.[95]

After this, three he-goats without any blemish are sacrificed to the deities by the priest on behalf of the people. The blood of the sacrificial animal is then sprinkled on the places dedicated for the deities. After this, the meat of the sacrificial animals is cooked and a part of it is first offered to the deities and the rest is eaten by the people and the priest.[96]

On Sunday morning, all the priests and the people bathe in the river and put on new clothes. The *Gisia* puts on a white *dhoti* and turban, about thirty feet in length, made of cotton or silk. The upper part of his body is left uncovered. *Zonthais* prepare a place each for their own deities and place plantain leaves, on which the blood of the sacrificial animals are to be sprinkled and the sacrificial meat is to be offered.[97] No idol or image is to be found, however, the deities are represented by small lumps of clay which are known as *Shaukhuli*.[98]

After all preparations have been made, the *Zonthais* begin invoking their own deities to come and accept the sacrificial offering. At this time the *Dainyas* assisted by *Baroas* sacrifice buffaloes and

[94] Daulagupu, Interview…

[95] Warisa, Interview…

[96] Lalsim, *Tribes…*, 22.

[97] Chatry, *Significance…*

[98] Although no idols or images are found, the deities are represented by small mounds of clay and sometimes clay figurines representing the deities and animals are also made. This is known as *Shaukhuli* which means "replica".

he-goats. The sacrificial blood is sprinkled on the plantain leaves laid out for the deities. K. Daulagupu says that in every sacrificial place, 2 buffaloes, 60 he-goats and 12 fowls are required.[99] On the other hand, Chatry writes that, in *Abungbra Madaikho* alone, 3 buffaloes, 60 he-goats and fowls are sacrificed, while in *Mahurbra Madaikho*, 3 buffaloes, 25 he-goats and fowls are sacrificed, and in *Dugubra* 1 buffalo, 15 he-goats and fowls are sacrificed.[100] The sacrificial ritual begins at *Abungbra Madaikho*, followed by the other two *Madaikhos*, the ritual ends at the same time.

Nobody is allowed to eat anything until all sacrificial rituals have been completed. After the completion of all rites and rituals, the meat offered to the deities is taken and distributed among the people by the priest as the divine favour called *misu*. Then the people eat the meat of the sacrificial animals with *Zu*[101] and cooked rice. This feast is called *melphaiba*.[102]

On the day of *Misengba* sacrifice, the people remaining in the villages also take bath in the morning and observe a half holy-day and do not perform any work and do not undertake any journey till noon. On Monday, i.e. a day after the sacrifice, all the people return to their respective villages with the *dithar* and distribute it to all the people of the village. The *dithar* purifies the entire village community from every impurity.

After all the people have returned to their villages, another feast is held in the house of the *Zonthai* or *Khunang*. In this, every member of the village community, including women and children are allowed to participate. The priests are given gifts like traditional cloth (*rithar*) as a gift which is called *khilimphai*. The gifts also include cash and kind. The priests do not take offence even if no gift is offered to them.[103]

---

[99] Daulagupu, Interview…

[100] Chatry, *Significance…*

[101] *Zu* is the traditional rice beer brewed locally by the Dimasa Kacharis. It is an indispensable item in their sacrifices, festivals and other ceremonies.

[102] *Melphaiba* actually means ceremonial feasting together for better relationship with each other and the deities. It is a reminder to the people to forget all kinds of enmities, grumblings and alterations among themselves. See Chatry, *Significance…*

[103] Lalsim, *Tribes…*, 23-24.

ii) *Krongfanggarba* (Sacrifice for welfare, protection of the village and good harvest)

Krongfanggarba[104] is an annual agricultural sacrifice which is performed just before the starting of sowing of crops according to the convenience of the concerned village.

It is usually observed at night and it goes on till noon of the next day sometime during January-February. According to K. Daulagupu, *Krongfanggarba* is observed on Mondays or Fridays only. Moreover, sacrifices are not to be offered on new moon nights.[105] On this day, the village deities as well as the *Khunang's* ancestral family deities are worshipped.

a) Purpose

Krongfanggarba is performed to ensure the welfare and protection of the entire village. Bordoloi writes that, *Krongfanggarba* is performed for the general prosperity of the village, a bumper harvest in cultivation and for the protection of the people from diseases and other natural calamities.[106] B.B. Kumar also states that, it is performed for plentiful crops and prosperity, and protection of the people from natural calamities and diseases.[107]

b) Preparations

In order to meet the expenses for this sacrifice, each family has to contribute something which is determined at a meeting of the village elders held at the courtyard of the village *Nodrang* (Bachelor's Dormitory). A male pig, 1 chicken and a fowl are required. Furthermore, eggs as demanded by the priest are also necessary.

---

[104] *Krongfanggarba* is also known as *Rajini Garba* or *Horni Garba*. The celebration that takes place at day time is known as *Rajini Garba* and the celebration that takes place at night is called is called *Horni Garba*

[105] Daulagupu, Interview...

[106] Bordoloi, *The Dimasa Kacharis...*, 97.

[107] B.B. Kumar, *The Tribal Societies of India: A Macro Perception* (New Delhi: Omsons Publications, 1998), 218.

Besides these sacrificial animals, 3 *Laothaisa*[108] and 15 plantain leaves are also required for the sacrifice. *Zu* is a necessity, although it is for the deities and not for human consumption. Crushed rice (*Hon*) is also necessary. For the act of sacrifice, 2 *Hojais* and 1 *Baroa* are required. A *Hojai* and a *Barao* perform sacrifice of the pig while another *Hojai* sacrifices the fowl.[109] When the date and time for the sacrifice have been fixed by the *Sali*,[110] the people are informed through the village herald (*Dilik*).[111]

On the morning of the appointed day, the *Khunang* or *Hojai* takes bath and after purifying himself he puts on a single white loincloth called *Rithar*. He then performs *Lamphungba*[112] to close the village roads leading to the village. In this sacrifice, three sticks of bamboo are fixed cross-wise, then an egg is split and seven deep marks are made on the ground with the sacrificial sword called *Seng*. When this has been done, the *Dilik* again announces that the ritual performance has begun and no one from the village should go out or do any work.

During the observance of the sacrificial rituals neither outsiders nor relatives are permitted to enter the village. All incoming and outgoing, settling in the village or shifting to another village must be done before the commencement of the sacrificial rituals. However, a little leniency is shown to the sick.[113]

c) *Krongfanggarba* Sacrifice

After the *Lamphungba* has been completed, all the male members of the village assemble at the ceremonial place prepared in the jungle. Some plantain leaves are spread on the sacrificial ground and bamboo

---

[108] *Laothaisa* is a bottle gourd pot used in offering rice beer. Offering someone rice beer in a *Laothaisa* is considered a sign of respect. Therefore, this particular pot plays an important role in the Dimasa Kachari festivals, marriage and sacrifices.

[109] Daulagupu, Interview...

[110] *Sali* is the village council responsible for the entire administration of the village. It consists of several officials and is headed by the *Khunang*.

[111] Lalsim, *Tribes...*, 24.

[112] *Lamphungba* is the ceremonial closing of the village road by offering a sacrifice. It is performed to prevent evil spirits from entering the village.

[113] Sajal Bathari, Interview...

sticks are fixed. On these bamboo sticks some pieces of cotton threads soaked in mustard oil are placed. The cotton threads are then lighted and the deities are invoked to show the sign whether they are pleased or not. If the deities are pleased, the wicks will be completely consumed, if not the wicks will go off immediately. This is a sort of divination which shows whether the year will be a prosperous one or not.[114]

The priest then cuts the egg and offers a prayer. Then the sacrificial pig is offered which is followed by the fowl. The raw as well as cooked sacrificial meat is offered to the deities by the priest. After this the sacrificial meat is taken by the villagers.[115] The priest does not eat anything till the ceremonial activities of the morning have been finished. At night, the ceremonial rituals are performed again as it was done in the morning. This is followed by feasting and drinking of *Zu*.

During the performance of this sacrifice, cultural activities such as singing or dancing are not performed. The restrictions are observed till noon the next day and during this time no activity except cooking, eating and fetching of water are allowed. When the time of restriction is over, the *Khunang* announces that the ceremonial rituals are over and the roads are opened and life returns back to normal.

iii) *Maisalaigarba* (Sacrifice for community welfare and good harvest)

"Mai" literally means "paddy". *Maisalaigarba* is an agricultural sacrifice which is observed before the ripening of paddy. The date for the sacrifice and the amount to be contributed by each family to meet the expenses of the sacrifice is fixed by the *Sali*.

a) Purpose:

Daulagupu says that it is an annual sacrifice which is offered for the welfare of the whole village, and only after the observance of this ceremony the villagers may eat the harvest.[116] Bathari also says that

[114] Chatry, *Significance...*

[115] Daulagupu, Interview...

[116] Daulagupu, Interview...

the sacrifice is offered for a good harvest.[117] The sacrifice is observed on Tuesdays or Fridays during September-October.

b) Preparations

A minimum of 16 chickens are required for this sacrifice.[118] Other sacrificial items are similar with the items required in the *Krongfanggarba* sacrifice. The sacrificial ritual is done in the morning and no one is allowed to enter the village till noon. All the necessary items for the sacrificial rituals are collected by the youths of the village on the previous day before the sacrifice.

c) *Maisalaigarba* Sacrifice

On the appointed day, the villagers along with the necessary sacrificial items proceed to the sacrificial place that has already been selected. On reaching the place, the *Hojai* takes bath and consecrates the place for the deities. He spreads plantain leaves and places a *longkhai* on the ground. On the plantain leaves, young paddy and the blood of the sacrificial animals are offered. At the same time, the priest implores the deities to accept the offerings and bless the *jhum*. The basket, which is used by the people for harvesting is probably placed to beseech the deities to fill it with a bountiful harvest. In this ritual, the evil spirits called *Sakainjiks*[119] are also pacified by offering the blood of the sacrificial animals to prevent them from harming the crops.

In this ceremony a small living chicken is also offered to the water deities. The chicken is put in a small boat made of plantain leaf and it is placed on the river. The children are asked to pelt stones

[117] Sajal Bathari, Interview...

[118] The number of chickens depends upon the smallness or largeness of the concerned village as all the people are to take part in the feast.

[119] *Sakainjiks* are the most feared malevolent spirits. *Sakainjik* is a generic term for a group of dreaded female spirits. In many ways *Sakainjiks* are similar to witches. The *Sakainjik* power is operated through a mortal female. Dr. Babul Roy is of the opinion that *Sakainjiks* are more like other evil female spirits believed by the Dimasa Kacharis; and, it is only recently that *Sakainjiks* have assumed some witch characteristics. See Babul Roy, "Descent Groupings, Belief System and Social Structure among the Dimasa Kacharis of Assam," *Man in India* 82/1&2, (2002): 73-99.

at it in order to make it sink. Through this, it is believed that the water deities would be appeased. The water deities are propitiated in order to get enough rain for the paddy to grow and bring a bountiful harvest.[120]

After all ceremonies and rituals have been completed, the sacrificial meat is cooked and a small part is offered to the deities. After this, the people start feasting together. They return to the village in the evening and the day of the sacrifice is observed as a holy day and the villagers abstain from any kind of activity.

iv) *Sengphong Nimadai* (Sacrifice offered to Clan Deity)

As has been identified earlier, the Dimasa Kacharis have 40 male clans known as *Sengphong.* Each *Sengphong* worships a different deity. Thus, *Sengphong Nimadai* is a sacrifice offered to the clan deity by the members of that particular patriclan.

There is no fixed time for the offering of this sacrifice. The clan members consult among themselves and if they feel that they have not performed this sacrifice for quite a long time, they can perform the sacrifice. There are 40 *Sengphongs* and the sacrificial animals as well as the sacrificial rituals differ according to the clan. It is performed during the morning time in the jungle. The expenses for the sacrifice are borne by the patriclan members with contributions. The sacrificial meat is returned to the village and eaten by all, including women and children. There are some clans where during the offering of their clan sacrifice, members of other clans cannot join.[121]

v) *Busu* (Harvest Festival which implies Sacrifice)

Busu may not be termed as a sacrifice in the strict sense. It is more of a socio-cultural harvest festival. However, sacrifices constitute an indispensable part of the *Busu* celebration and the celebration would be incomplete and meaningless without the sacrifices. In this section the cultural as well as the religious aspect of the *Busu* celebration has been highlighted.

[120] Lalsim, *Tribes...*, 27.

[121] Sajal Bathari, Interview...

The *Busu* may be celebrated at any period from the end of winter to the beginning of the rainy season.[122]

a) Different types of *Busu*

Writers like Bordoloi are of the opinion that the *Busu* festival may be divided into two (2) categories.[123] On the other hand writers like Ramdina Lalsim and Palon Ch. Warisa and other knowledgeable Dimasa Kacharis living in Dima Hasao are of the opinion that there are three (3) types of *Busu.*[124] The present writer, is compliant with the view of Lalsim and Warisa, hence the three (3) categories of *Busu* are discussed in the following way.

b) *Busu Jidap*

Busu Jidap is observed for three days. It is celebrated under the guidance of the *Khunang*. The first day is called *mi-staiba*, which means slaughtering day of animals for feast. The animals are slaughtered in the morning and in the afternoon, a community feast called *Khalaima khamba* is held in the house of the *Khunang*. When the sun sets, the competition called *Baiba Bdailaiba* which consists of singing, dancing are held in the courtyard of the *Nodrang*. The whole night is spent in dancing and merry making.[125]

The second day is called *Busuma*, which means the main *Busu* day. On this day children or the youths pay respect and homage

---

[122] Even though *Busu* may be celebrated at any convenient time, since 1994 as per the decision of the Dimasa Kachari community of Dima Hasao, the Autonomous Council had officially declared 27th January as Busu festival day. See Choudhury, *Folklore...*; Lalsim, *Tribes...*

[123] According to Bordoloi, when it is observed for three or five days it is *Surem* and when it is observed for seven days it is called *Hangseu Manaoba*. He further writes that *Surem* is simply an abbreviated form of *Hangseu Manaoba*. See Bordoloi, *The Dimasa Kacharis...*, 93.

[124] According to these people, the three (3) types of *Busu* are; i) When the *Busu* is celebrated for three days, it is called *Busu Jidap* ii) When it is observed for five days, it is called *Surem Baino* and, iii) When it is observed for seven days it is called *Hangseu Manaoba*. Lalsim, *Tribes...*; Warisa, Interview...

[125] Lalsim, *Tribes...*, 28.

to their parents and their elders either individually or collectively.[126] The whole day is spent in eating and drinking *Zu*.

On the third and last day, young boys and girls pay a house to house visit of the selected well-to-do persons of the village, singing and dancing in their courtyards. Whatever they collect either in cash or kind from this is used for the feast. In the evening or at dawn as per the instructions of the village priest, they end their merry-making. On behalf of the village, the priest then performs a sacrifice on the main road of the village by sacrificing a fowl to the village deity for any fault done during the festival. This sacrificial ritual marks the end of festivities.[127]

c) *Surem Baino*

Surem Baino is generally celebrated for five days. Unlike the *Busu Jidap*, it is celebrated under the guidance of a selected leader called *Gajaibao*. The *Gajaibao* is supposed to be selected well in advance. All activities are done in the courtyard of the *Gajaibao*. These are the main differences between *Busu Jidap* and *Surem Baino*.[128]

d) *Hangseu Manaoba*

The first two categories of *Busu* are celebrated widely by villages. However, the third and grandest category, *Hangseu Manaoba* is mostly celebrated by a large village where there are a large number of youths as it involves time, energy and huge expenditures. Bordoloi writes that, even though *Busu* is a community festival for the entire village, nonetheless it is the youths of the village who have to bear the entire responsibility of the celebration of this festival.[129] The responsibility of fund collection and collection of all necessary materials is endured by the youths.

At the time of *Hangseu Manaoba* the erection of the *Fangsla* at the entrance of the village before the start of the ceremonies is very

---

[126] This ceremonial blessing is called *Busu Gaba* and is usually done before mid-noon.

[127] Lalsim, *Tribes...*, 29.

[128] Tapadar, comp., *Festivals...*, 17.

[129] Bordoloi, *The Dimasa Kacharis...*, 92-93.

important. The sacrificial buffalo is made to pass through this gate and circumambulate it. This intricate and artistic gate is wholly made from bamboo and it demonstrates the artistic skill of the Dimasa Kacharis.

During the celebration period, the village observes holidays called *Genna*, meaning restricted holiday. During the celebration no one is supposed to go out for work or on a journey, everyone must try his/her level best to make the celebration a grand success. The celebrations of *Hangseu Manaoba* are held under the leadership of the *Gajaibao*. Besides this leader, there is also a boy leader called *Nagahoja* and a girl leader called *Mathlarao*.

The first day of the *Hangseu Manaoba* is called *Hangseu Busu Rajini Sthaiba.*[130] In the morning, the village deities are pacified by offering sacrifices either of pigs, fowls or goats by the elders. Although, the principal deity of a village differs from village to village, *Sibrai* is remembered by all, as he is considered to be the main deity. The deities are offered sacrifices to bless the celebration of the festival so that no accident or any untoward incident takes place during the time of celebration. After the sacrificial ritual is over, a portion of the sacrificial meat is cooked in the house of the *Khunang* or *Gajaibao*, and the rest is distributed to each household according to their contribution. Then the village elders would feast together by eating the sacrificial meat and drinking rice beer. The youths and children are prohibited from taking part in this feast as it is a purely sacramental one. It is called *midogarba.*[131]

The second day is called *Nagaraoni Sithaiba.*[132] In the morning the buffalo which was solely bought by the youth members is killed and a portion is prepared for their feast and the rest is distributed to the youth members. Before they eat the cooked meat, a handful is offered to *Sibrai*. While the meat is offered to *Sibrai*, the following sacred song is pronounced by everyone so that they may have a blessed *Busu.*[133]

---

[130] This means the slaughtering day of animals by the village elders.

[131] Tapadar, comp., *Festivals...*, 18.

[132] This means slaughtering day of the animals by the youths.

[133] Lalsim, *Tribes...*, 32.

Ningmaijing ang maijing Saimaiba
Sibrai ribani saimaiba
Saijer unijang saimaiba
Uyaidananag adungrau Uyaidanang
Baithelik baihining lailade[134]

English version:

> The auspicious day has appeared in our lives not because of our wishes, but because of Sibrai. The day has dawned after a long time, let this day not pass by in vain brothers and sisters. Let us dance, and continue dancing with happiness.[135]

This is followed with a community feast in honour of the *Gajaibao* and the *Hangseu* (youth association), which is called *Suba jiba*. The day is spent in eating, drinking and merriment. At sunset, the youths hold a community singing fellowship called *Bagaoba*. This fellowship also takes the form of a procession. This procession is a call to the community members to forgive all debts and forget every grievance, differences and enmity and join in the festivities. Chatry also marks that, only when the people have one mind and one thought then the festival brings happiness to them, and it will become a success.[136]

The third day called *Busuma* is the main *Busu* day and it begins with a ceremonial paying of homage and respect to the elders by the children, individually or collectively. The elders are also presented with gifts such as a handful of cooked meat and a cup full of rice beer. On this day, the Dimasa Kacharis pay homage to the living; they also give food and drink as the last offering to the spirits of the dead of the previous year. This last offering is called *Makhamgarkhaoba*. Bordoloi also asserts this religio-cultural practice by saying:

> On this very day, the ritual called *Makhamgarkhaoba*, meaning the last offering of food and drink to the dead of the preceding year,

---

[134] Zahid Ahmed Tapadar, *Dimasa Anvesa* (Haflong: Nikhil Bharat Banga Sahitya Sammelan, 1996), 43. Hereafter cited as Tapadar, *Dimasa Anvesa...*

[135] Tapadar, *Dimasa Anvesa...*, 43.

[136] Chatry, *Significance...*

has to be performed with a view to sever the tie between the dead and the living.[137]

A community feast is also arranged on this day. Every family entertained people in the house with a handful of meat in a plantain and a bamboo cup of *Zu*. In the afternoon, traditional sports are held in the spirit of friendship and understanding and to entertain the people. The night is spent in singing, dancing and merry-making.

The fourth, fifth and sixth days are called *Baikhaoba* or *Jikhaoba*.[138] On these days too community feasts are held and the days are spent mainly in eating, drinking, singing and dancing. Every family entertains guests and friends with rice beer, meat and food. Bordoloi perceives:

> The wealthy people entertain lavishly the co-villagers and guests with meat, food and drinks to their hearts' content. This is done with a view to enhance the prestige and social status of the family. Higher the number of guests entertained, higher would soar prestige and social status of the family members. Thus every well-to-do family has a tendency to spend about one half of their annual production of food during the observance of the Bishu festival itself.[139]

On the sixth afternoon all the guests, friends and relatives are to leave the village. In the evening after all the outsiders leave the village some youths jokingly pull out the main door of the *Gajaibao's* house and throw it into the river, and replace it with a new one. This is known as *derga khouma*.[140] At night sacrifices are performed by offering chickens to the village deities.

On the seventh and last day of the *Busu*, the entire people of the village perform a *Garba*.[141] It is more or less a purification ritual observed with a view to purify the village from any kind of impurity

---

[137] Bordoloi, *The Dimasa Kacharis*..., 94.

[138] Tapadar, *Dimasa Anvesa*..., 43.

[139] Bordoloi, *The Dimasa Kacharis*..., 95.

[140] It means "the door is pulled off". The pulling out of the door may symbolise the end of the *Gajaibao's* responsibility.

[141] *Garba* literally means "worship day" or "sacrificial day".

that may have been incurred during *Busu* due to the presence of many outsiders. Hence, the presence of any outsider during the performance of this *Garba* is considered taboo. During this ritual no one is allowed to enter or go out of the village.[142]

In this ritual eggs and chickens are sacrificed to the deities on the approach roads to the village and the roads are blocked by fixing two bamboo sticks crosswise to warn any outsider of the ongoing *Garba* sacrifice.

3. INDIVIDUAL SACRIFICES

Among the Dimasa Kacharis, there is nothing like a village shrine or place of worship. The individuals perform different rituals and sacrifices for general welfare of the family or for getting cured from an ailment. The Dimasa Kacharis believe that numerous deities and spirits constantly get involved in their life. Hence, in order to coexist harmoniously with these deities and spirits, they have to please and appease them constantly with ritual offerings and sacrifices.

i) *Naisodi-Nusodi* and *Nanadihangba* (Pregnancy and Birth Sacrifices)

During pregnancy, the husband has an important role to play as he has to worship *Naisodi-Nusodi*[143] by sacrificing a hen. After a child is born, the attending midwife known as *Hojaijule* along with her assistant known as *Barwaju* go to a nearby river and perform a sacrifice by breaking an egg and takes bath in order to purify themselves. *Sibrai* is also worshipped for the wellbeing of the newborn.[144] The Dimasa Kacharis believe that rivers are the abodes of evil spirits. Hence, this sacrifice is done in order to protect the mother and the baby from the wrath of these evil spirits.

The ceremony of bringing the baby outside the four walls of the house, called *Nanadihangba* is performed only after the umbilical cord falls off. The father has to sacrifice a cock and a hen and a feast

[142] Bordoloi, *The Dimasa Kacharis...*, 95-96.

[143] *Naisodi-Nusodi* is considered to be the deity of child welfare and it is believed that by worshipping her one can be assured of safe and easy child birth.

[144] Bordoloi, *The Dimasa Kacharis...*, 49.

has to be offered. Puffed rice and a drop of rice beer on a fingertip are also placed into the mouth of the baby.[145] On this day the head of the baby is shaved. This ceremonial shaving is a must in the Dimasa Kachari society and it is known as *Khanaigusugarba*.[146]

Bisht and Bankoti discern that not all are able to perform *Nanadihangba* and it is also not obligatory. Hence, only those who can afford, perform this ceremony. A feast is held and friends and relatives are invited and *Zu* and pork or other meat, except beef, is offered to the guests.[147]

ii) *Mayofagarba, Lamphungba, Midogarba* and *Madaikhilimba* (Sacrifices connected with Marriage)

In the traditional Dimasa Kachari marriage, on the day of the marriage the bridegroom has to go to the bride's village. Before going his father performs a sacrifice known as *Mayofagarba* in presence of the village elders for safe journey of his son. *Mayofagarba* is a sacrifice offered to all deities. It is a multi-purpose sacrifice which is performed on the eve of a journey for ceremonial purposes, for good and healthy livestock, for bountiful harvest and so on. If the sacrifice is offered for good harvest, it is offered before sowing of the seed. There is no fixed time for other purposes, but it is to be offered as the occasion demands.

In this sacrifice, it is not compulsory to employ a priest because the sacrifice can be offered by householder. The sacrificial victim is 1 hen that has not laid an egg. The sacrifice is performed inside the house near the main door. A *khapra*[148] is made and the incantations are chanted; then the hen is killed and the blood is sprinkled on the

---

[145] Bordoloi, *The Dimasa Kacharis…*, 50.

[146] If the baby is a male, the father or a senior male member belonging to the father's clan performs this task of shaving. In case of a female baby, the mother or the father may perform the task. It is prohibited for the mother or women to shave the head of a male baby. If they do, the boy will not be allowed to worship the Dimasa Kachari deities. See. Bordoloi, *The Dimasa Kacharis…* ; Danda, *Among the Dimasa…*

[147] Narendra S. Bisht and T.S. Bankoti, *Encyclopaedic Ethnography of the Himalayan Tribes: A-D, Vol. 1* (New Delhi: Global Vision Pub House, 2004), 96.

[148] A plate made with bamboo and covered with plantain leaves.

plantain leaves. The sacrificial meat is then cooked and eaten by the family members.[149]

The Dimasa Kacharis believe that malevolent spirits hovering in the air would try to disturb them as they go on a journey for ceremonial purposes. If *Mayofagarba* is performed, the benevolent deities would protect them from the attack of malevolent spirits

Before entering the bride's village, the groom's father performs another sacrifice by cutting an egg. This is known as *lamphungba* which means "to close the road". According to the traditional Dimasa Kachari belief, evil spirits are constantly hovering in the air and if *lamphungba* is not performed these evil spirits may accompany the groom's party and enter the village. Hence, *lamphungba* is performed to prevent evil spirits from entering the village.

The next sacrifice is called *midogarba.* In this sacrifice, a pig is offered in honour of the deities. It is believed that the newlywed couple may have a prosperous life through the performance of this sacrifice. This sacrifice is performed for the welfare of the new couple in order to get the blessings of the deities.

After staying at the bride's place for a few days, the new couple travels to the groom's place. On this journey again *mayofagarba* and *lamphungba* sacrifices are performed; but this time by the bride's father. After the couple stay in the groom's village *madaikhilimba*[150] is performed by the groom's father. After this sacrifice, the bride officially becomes a member of her husband's patriclan. In this sacrifice, either a he-goat or a fowl is sacrificed to the clan deities.[151]

iii) *Maimutharba* (Sacrifice connected with Death)

The Dimasa Kacharis usually practice cremation. Soon after a person dies, a cock is sacrificed by a male member of the family near the head of the deceased. It is believed that the sacrificed cock will show the deceased the right way to heaven. Before the deceased is taken to the cremation ground called *Mangphlang* the body is bathed

---

[149] Sajal Bathari, Interview...

[150] *Madaikhilimba* means the worship of clan deities

[151] Daulagupu, Interview...

ceremonially and then placed on a bier (*Bangfong*) made of split bamboos.[152]

The traditional Dimasa Kacharis believe that death in the family makes the paddy polluted. Hence, *Maimutharba*[153] sacrifice has to be performed to purify the paddy. There is no fixed time for the performance of the *Maimutharba* sacrifice. It depends upon the economic condition of the family.

If only one bamboo is used for making the bier, then in the *Maimutharba* sacrifice, a pig has to be offered and the four persons carrying the bier will get a leg of the sacrificed pig. If more than one bamboo is used in making the bier, two buffaloes have to be sacrificed and the legs will be given to the persons carrying the bier.[154]

iv) *Majhai Khilingba and Langlai* (Agricultural Sacrifices)

Every Dimasa Kachari family offers a sacrifice called *Majhai Khilingba* before the cultivating of the *jhum* site. In this sacrificial ritual, a hen is offered. It is done in order to bring blessings upon the land that they are going to cultivate. After this, to begin cultivation, another ritual known as *Langlai* is performed. In this, a cock, two hens and three eggs are required. The sacrifices are offered in the jungle. The *Hojai* invokes the deity *Langlai* to protect the *jhum* from natural calamities, wild animals, insects, etc., and to bless it with a bumper harvest.[155]

v) *Naijuni Khilimba* (Sacrifice for Development and Prosperity)

a) Purpose and Preparations

Naijuni Khilimba is a family sacrifice which is offered for the overall development and prosperity of the family. It is usually offered at dawn. In this sacrifice 1 chicken is required. The services of a priest

---

[152] The number of bamboos used in the making of this bier shows the social status of the deceased. If the deceased is poor, then only one bamboo is used.

[153] In Dimasa Kachari *Mai* means paddy and *tharba* means purification. Therefore, *Maimutharba* means "purification of paddy."

[154] Bordoloi, *The Dimasa Kacharis…*, 62.

[155] Daulagupu, Interview…

may not be required if the householder knows the process of offering the sacrifice. The wife may act as the helper. In this sacrifice, any outsider, even close relatives are not allowed to participate. The sacrificial meat is taken by the family members alone. The sacrifice is offered outside the house near a river. The frequency of the sacrifice is determined by the *phatri* or the householder himself, if he knows the process.[156]

b) *Naijuni Khilimba* Sacrifice

In this sacrifice, besides the sacrificial animals, plantain leaves with the pointed sides all facing towards the same side, stitched together with a bamboo are required. At the sacrificial place, 7 such plantain leaves are kept in the middle and 5 each on the left and right. After all preparations have been made the priest or the householder cuts an egg while taking bath in the river and chants an incantation. The cutting of an egg and taking of bath signifies the washing away of all impurities. After taking bath, the sacrificial animal is killed and the blood is sprinkled on the banana leaves. The blood must be sprinkled first on the middle plantain leaves. During the sprinkling of the sacrificial blood some incantations are chanted. Then the sacrificial meat is cooked and eaten by the family members.[157]

The door of the house is closed before leaving for the sacrificial ceremony and it remains closed and cannot be opened by the members of the family. It has to be opened by a well-to-do woman of the village adorned in all her finery, who is usually informed beforehand by the family for this auspicious ceremony. The rationale behind this is that development and prosperity may enter the home.

If bad luck and misfortune continue to befall upon the family even after the offering of this sacrifice the *Phatri* is consulted to know what exactly the deities or spirits demand. Then the sacrifice is repeated in accordance with the fresh prescription of the *Phatri*.[158] If the family fails to offer the fresh prescribed sacrifice, more misfortunes may befall upon them.

[156] Sajal Bathari, Interview...

[157] Sajal Bathari, Interview...

[158] Sajal Bathari, Interview...

vi) Curative Sacrifices

As has been pointed out in Chapter Two Section 5 (iv), the traditional Dimasa Kacharis believe in the existence of numerous malevolent spirits who are responsible for causing sicknesses, misfortunes and calamities. These malevolent spirits, born of the seventh egg of *Arikhidima*, are believed as being ordained by *Sibrai* to inhabit the valleys, streams, rivers and any other natural objects. In order to be free from the attack of these malevolent spirits they need to be constantly appeased through the offering of sacrifices.

a) Malevolent Spirits and their respective required sacrificial items

Even though there are several malevolent spirits believed to cause sickness, only the common malevolent spirits and their respective required sacrificial items are mentioned here below:[159]

Table 1: Showing the common malevolent spirits and their respective sacrificial items

Sl. No.	Name of Spirits	Sacrificial Items
1.	*Bairagi*	Hen-2, duck-1, egg-3
2.	*Daujidaimba*	Egg-15/30, etc.
3.	*Daujar*	Hen-2, egg-2
4.	*Dakhinsa*	Hen-9, egg-3
5.	*Dikhongnami*	Pig-1, hen-1, duck-1 plus egg according to the number of family members
6.	*Jompara*	Hen-1, cock-1, pigeon-2
7.	*Hagrani*	Either hen-1; or hen-2, duck-1; or hen-3, egg-3
8.	*Haklini*	Pig-1, cock-1
9.	*Halebdi*	Hen-1

[159] Babul Roy and A.N.M. Irshad Ali, "Medical Pluralism and Acceptance of the Different Medical Options among the Dimasa Kacharis of North Cachar Hills in Assam," *Journal of Human Ecology* 12/1 (2001): 27.

10.	*Hapai*	Either duck-1, hen-2, egg-1, chicken-3; or duck-1, hen-2, egg-4
11.	*Haremdi*	Goat-1, hen-2, egg-10
12.	*Khorongbaji*	Pig-1, hen-1, cock-1
13.	*Khorongner*	Pig-1
14.	*Londisa*	Hen-5
15.	*Madaima*	Hen-3
16.	*Mungreng*	Goat-1, chicken-2
17.	*Padumaniban*	Goat-1, hen-5, pigeon-2, egg-5
18.	*Sani*	Either goat-1, hen-1, egg-4; or goat-1, duck-1, cock-1
19.	*Singkharao*	Goat-1
20.	*Sakainjik*	Either goat-1, hen-1, egg-10; or hen-1, duck-1
21.	*Shegainlambra*	Hen-1, egg-2
22.	*Simangkhuba*	Pig-1

The above table clearly shows the huge pantheon of malevolent spirits that need to be constantly appeased through the offering of sacrifices as well as the huge amount of money required for buying the sacrificial items.[160]

b) Diagnosis of sickness through divination

Due to the constraint of time and space, only the method of divination by using a bamboo stick may be mentioned here. When a person falls ill, he/she goes to a *Gorashali*. The *Gorashali* cuts a bamboo into two halves with the ends pointed. Then he says "If the spirit causing the sickness is a male, let the bamboo fall like this," then he drops the two bamboo sticks on the ground. If the bamboo does not fall in the way mentioned by the *Gorashali*, it means that the spirit is a female. After the *Gorashali* identifies whether the spirit causing the sickness is a male or female spirit, he continues to ask

[160] In Haflong market, one hen costs approximately Rs. 400-500, one goat costs approximately Rs. 6,000-8,000, one full-grown pig costs approximately Rs. 20,000-25,000. Not all Dimasa Kachari families rear enough livestock to meet the huge demands made by the sacrifices. So they have to eventually buy the sacrificial animals; this has a serious impact upon their economy.

questions by dropping the bamboo sticks again and again to find out the required sacrificial prescription.[161]

After the diagnosis has been completed, the person goes to the *Hojai* who performs the required sacrifice. When minor ailments get cured in their own natural course, they attribute it as an act of kindness of the deity or spirit. If the sick person does not recover after the first sacrifice, then it is referred back to the *Gorashali* for fresh diagnosis and then again referred back to the *Hojai* for the performance of the sacrifice. If the patient does not recover the process goes on and on, and if all else fails the beleaguered sick person or his/her family members go to the *Phatri* to know what the deity wants to tell them.[162] The ineffectiveness of such sacrifices does not induce the traditional Dimasa Kacharis to stop offering sacrifices or to give up their traditional faith. Danda affirms this by stating with the following:

> More often it happens that in spite of repeated offerings to the deities the patient did not improve or survive. The ineffectiveness of worship for curing disease does not make any crack in their traditional faith over the supernatural agencies.[163]

c) Sacrifice offered to *Shegainlambra* a female spirit

The method of sacrifice and the sacrificial animals and other items depends upon the spirit causing the sickness. Since it would be impossible to mention all the methods of sacrifices, in this section only the method of sacrifice offered to *Shegainlambra* a female spirit has been mentioned.

After proper divination by a *Gorashali*, the family of the sick person arranges a sacrifice for the spirit of *Shegainlambra*. The sacrifice is offered in the afternoon on the way to the river. The offerings required are 1 hen and 2 eggs. Besides these, a lit lamp (*thaopari*) and a *karma* (a kind of stinging plant) is planted at the sacrificial place as a symbol of the spirit. Then, the priest offers the

---

[161] Sajal Bathari, Interview…

[162] Denon Naiding, Interview…

[163] Danda, *Among the Dimasa…*, 129.

sacrificial animal and eggs to the spirit while chanting incantations. Although the sacrificial meat is taken by the people present there, fried egg as well as a small portion of the sacrificial meat is also offered to the spirit.[164]

4. CONCLUDING REMARKS

Tribal religion is often said to begin from the womb till death. This is proved by the Dimasa Kachari traditional religion with its innumerable rites and rituals. Many of the community sacrifices are connected with their agricultural life. Even though the various sacrifices of the Dimasa Kacharis are related to agriculture, they are also deeply religious in nature because most of them begin with a sacrificial ritual and conclude with a sacrificial ritual.

In spite of the influence of modernization and Brahmanical Hinduism, although many of the urbanized Dimasa Kacharis have begun neglecting the observance of many of these sacrificial rituals, credit goes to the Dimasa Kacharis living in rural Dima Hasao for preserving these age-old traditional beliefs and practices. Therefore, it would do well for the present-day Dimasa Kacharis to preserve and treasure these ancient rites and rituals as they are the ones that gives them their identity and provides them unity and occasions to worship as a community.

[164] Sarda Hojai, Interview...

Chapter 4

THE IMPACT OF SACRIFICES ON THE TRADITIONAL DIMASA KACHARIS

1. INTRODUCTION

From the previous chapter, one can discern that sacrifices occupy an integral part in the everyday lives of the traditional Dimasa Kacharis. Therefore, it is obvious that these sacrifices would have a deep impact on their socio-economic and religious life. Thus, this chapter is devoted at analyzing those various impacts.

2. SOCIO-ECONOMIC IMPACTS

Sacrifice being the basic rite through which a religion performs its function in society, it inevitably has social impacts. The various impacts of sacrifice on the socio-economic life of the traditional Dimasa Kacharis may be enumerated as follows:

i) Impact on Family

In order to co-exist harmoniously as a community, an individual must be prepared to sacrifice the family interest to the larger interest of the community; this forms the basis of communal life. In the tribal religion, individual life and community life are intricately intertwined. In order to be truly human, one must belong to the whole community including the ancestors and creation. Hence, every individual is expected to actively share in the beliefs, ceremonies, rituals and festivals of the community.

In the traditional Dimasa Kachari religion, the sacrifices demand every family to participate physically and financially in every community sacrifice that is held for the general welfare and prosperity of the community. In such community sacrifices, the people are expected to forget all enmity and bitterness that they may harbor against one another. They are expected to rise above their petty differences and work for the betterment of the society as a whole.

Moreover, the traditional sacrifices demand obedience from each and every family. On occasions of community sacrifice, a holy day is generally observed when no one is allowed to do any private or family work. Everyone is expected to observe the holy day for the good of the larger community.

The clan tie among the traditional Dimasa Kacharis, as has been mentioned, is so strong that an offence done to a clan member by an outsider is considered to be an offence against the whole clan. Hence, fulfillment of every clan obligation to the clan members is a must. Thus, during the sacrifice offered to the clan deity, all families belonging to that particular clan must participate and contribute something. The clan members are to be invited to the funeral sacrifice and feast or else it is considered a serious offence.

Therefore, one can say that, the sacrifices enable the traditional Dimasa Kacharis to rise above one's own interests for the larger interest of the community. Hence, one can affirm that, sacrifices have reinforced family and social unity to which all the individual members belong. They play an important role as a cohesive element for the family and the community. Through the sacrifices, the traditional Dimasa Kachari religion has been preserved and handed down orally from one generation to another.

ii) Impact upon the whole Dimasa Kachari Community

The traditional religion of the Dimasa Kacharis is basically a community religion which demands the active participation of every individual in the sacrificial rites, rituals and festivals.

During the observance of community sacrifices that are observed for the public welfare, the materials necessary for the sacrifice are collectively contributed by the community. These sacrifices are most often followed by a community feast in which all the members of the community participate. Every member of the community is anticipated to obey the orders of the community leaders, the oracles pronounced by the *Phatri*, or the instructions of the priests.

The people are also expected to maintain decorum and forget all enmities, rejoice in the blessings of the Supreme god (*Madai*) and seek his blessings for the general welfare of the community. They are expected to take an active part both physically and financially in all rituals due to their shared membership of the same community and religion. Due to their participation in such sacrifices with other members of the community, the traditional Dimasa Kacharis are facilitated to become conscious of their unity as members of one and the same community. This kind of kinship unity is affirmed by Emile Durkheim who asserts, "...they (community members) mutually show one another that they are all members of the same moral community and they become conscious of the kinship uniting them."[165]

Consequently, one can affirm that it is through the observance of the community sacrifices that social ties have been strengthened and reinforced among the traditional Dimasa Kacharis. The various community sacrifices unite the traditional Dimasa Kacharis and let them feel oneness with their fellow brothers and sisters with whom they maintain their religious identity and ethnicity. The sacrifices also provide continuity with the ancestors and the past. The various sacrifices are performed by the traditional Dimasa Kacharis because their ancestors did so. Hence, participation in the sacrifices affords the individuals and community continuity with the ancestors and provides a sense of social solidarity and unity.

Moreover, during the observance of the community sacrifices, especially *Busu*, the juniors of the community pay homage to the

---

[165] Emile Durkheim, "*The Elementary Forms of the Religious Life,*" translated by Joseph Ward Swain (London: George Allen & Unwin Ltd., 1915), 358. Hereafter cited as Durkheim, *Elementary Forms...*

elders by offering gifts and rice-beer and seek their blessings. This indicates that Dimasa Kachari believe that their foreparents or ancestors, to some extent, hold the power of blessing to the younger generations if they are well pleased. This is not a sacrifice; however it is ceremonial in nature and obligatory. Hence, we can also say that sacrifices also promote respect and reverence for the elders of the society by the young ones.

iii) Ecological Impact

Many of the sacrifices, especially the community sacrifices of the traditional Dimasa Kacharis are associated with the celebration of their socio-religious festivals which are connected with the land. Hence, it has been said that it is in the land and its resources that the tribal people built a culture-religious myths, rituals, ceremonies and social control mechanism.[166] Nirmal Minz also writes,

> ...a nature-human-spirit continuum is the key to the tribal vision of life. All religious rites, observances, festivities are based on this holistic vision of reality. Tribal religion accepts the integral relationships of nature, human and spirit in their experiences.[167]

The land is the source of life and sustenance for the tribal people. All their agricultural and pastoral occupations depend upon nature. The land with its myriad creation relates human beings to the Creator, God.[168] K. Thanzauva, a tribal theologian from North-East India has also expressed that, for tribals land is the source of life and is sacred, for there is no other temple except the land itself. It is the gift of God who also dwells in the land.[169]

---

[166] T. Vanlaltlani, *Tribal Religion...*, 16.

[167] Nirmal Minz, "The Study of Tribal Religion in India," in *Re-visioning India's Religious Traditions: Essays in Honour of Eric Lott*, edited by David C. Scott and Israel Selvanayagam (Delhi: ISPCK, 1996), 122.

[168] T. Vanlaltlani, *Tribal Religion...*, 15.

[169] K. Thanzauva, *Theology of Community: Tribal Theology in the Making* (Aizawl: Mizo Theological Conference, 1997), 173. Hereafter cited as K. Thanzauva, *Theology of Community...*

Due to the land-centered element of tribal religion, Presler and others have termed tribal religion as "nature religion,"[170] emphasizing the animistic character. However, tribal religion cannot be called nature religion even though great reverence is given to natural objects such as rivers, trees, mountains, etc. They are revered because they are believed to be inhabited by malevolent spirits and benevolent deities. It reminds them of the creative power of their god. K. Thanzauva further writes that, since tribals depend heavily upon the fertility of the soil, they develop a deep respect for the earth.[171]

Similarly, land for the Dimasa Kacharis is the gift of *Madai*, a source from which they get all things necessary for their survival. It is the source of all their religious beliefs and practices and their culture. All things required for their sacrificial rituals such as plantain leaves, rice, bamboos, animals, etc., are all provided from nature's bounty. The absence of even one sacrificial item would render the ritual incomplete and valueless. For the traditional Dimasa Kacharis, nature and creation are in one way or the other related to their religious beliefs and practices.

Even though they have no idea about the whereabouts of *Madai*, nature and creation reminds the traditional Dimasa Kacharis of the omnipresence of *Madai*. Due to their land-centered worldview, they offer sacrifices during community festivals to purify the land and the people, and make the land more productive. The sacrificial blood is offered not only to appease or propitiate the deities and spirits, it is also offered to the earth which is the source of their sustenance and livelihood.

The Dimasa Kacharis believe the whole Dimasa land to be the habitat of their six ancestral deities. The entire nature including trees, rocks and rivers is also considered as the habitat of benevolent deities as well as malevolent spirits. This belief of the traditional Dimasa Kacharis makes them very much, intentionally or unintentionally, conscious about the ecological concern. Even though they do not formulate eco-theology, their observance of many taboos and restrictions related to fishing, hunting, cultivation, cutting of trees,

---

[170] Presler, *Primitive Religion…*, 300.

[171] K. Thanzauva, *Theology of Community..*, 177.

etc., is very much dealing with ecological balance. These taboos in turn make the people cautious not to incur the wrath of the deities and spirits. When certain faults are committed by the people, sacrifices have to be offered to appease the angry deities or spirits. This animistic belief which results in the observance of sacrifices instills the traditional worldview upon the younger generation and inculcates sensitivity towards the eco-system.

iv) Impact on Sexual Promiscuity

An indispensable element of the sacrifices of the traditional Dimasa Kacharis is their traditional *Zu*. During the celebration of community sacrifices such as *Busu*, whole nights are spent in drinking *Zu* and dancing by the young men and women of the village.

According to Lalronghaka Ngamlai, the sacrifices indirectly promote sexual promiscuity among the youths. During the time of the festivals, due to the rampant use of liquor, sexual promiscuity among the youths is seen. This results in unwanted pregnancies and infanticides. Due to the rigid clan exogamy, not all sexual union can culminate in marriages. Hence, they have to resort to abortion, infanticides, and orphans.[172]

v) Impact on Gender Inequity

At the time of childbirth, the *Hojaijule* and *Barwaju*, the midwife and her assistant conduct everything, including the birth rituals. Therefore, these women are accorded high respect and honor in the Dimasa Kachari society.[173] Moreover, as has been mentioned, in some of the sacrifices offered by the family, even though the actual sacrifice is performed by the husband, the wife may also assist in the performance of the sacrificial ritual.

However, the women are prohibited from participating in the community sacrifices which are usually held in the jungles or near rivers. Even though they are allowed to participate in the community

---

[172] Interview with Lalronghaka Ngamlai, Ex-Evangelist and Pastor, resident of Haflong, 18 November 2013. Hereafter cited as Ngamlai, Interview…

[173] Suparna Barua, "A Woman in Dimasa Society-A Note", in *Communities of North-East India: An Anthropological Perspective*, edited by Farida Ahmed Das and Indira Barua (New Delhi: Mittal Publications, 1996), 149.

feast that is held when the sacrificial meat is brought back to the village, they are not allowed to participate in the actual sacrifice. Moreover, no female religious functionaries are found among the Dimasa Kacharis. Priesthood among the Dimasa Kacharis is the sole right of the menfolk. All religious rites and rituals of importance are performed by men. Hence, one can say that the sacrifices and the traditional religion of the Dimasa Kacharis as a whole promotes gender inequity and does gross injustice to the Dimasa Kachari women.

Sacrifices provide the community to perpetuate gender inequity and commit injustice towards the women. However, in Dimasa Kachari society, due to prevalence of dual descent system, women do not feel that they are subject to socio-religious injustice. But, there is the impression that a socio-religious atmosphere of equality does not exist among them. Their society is flexible but it does not make men and women equal. But, the women have a feeling of not being discriminated against.[174]

vi) Causal factors of Poverty

The various sacrifices are also causal factors of poverty among the traditional Dimasa Kacharis. According to Mr. Denon Naiding, there have been cases of entire families annihilated due to poverty as a result of the observance of the endless cycle of sacrifices.[175]

Table 2: Showing the traditional Dimasa Kachari opinion on the question of expensiveness/inexpensiveness of sacrifices

Different opinions	Respondents	Percentage
Expensive	47	67.14%
Inexpensive	12	17.14%
Having no opinion	11	15.71%
Total	**70**	**100%**

[174] Walter Fernandes, Melville Pereira and Vizalenu Khatso, "Gender Impact of Tribal Customary Laws in North Eastern India: A Summary of the Final Report," http://www.onlineministries.creighton.edu (20 July 2013).

[175] Denon Naiding, Interview…

The above table clearly indicates that 67.14% of the respondents expressed that the sacrifices are expensive, while only 17.14% feel that they are inexpensive. There are 15.71% who do not have any opinion. This table shows the expensiveness of the sacrifices and if sacrifices were not necessary, it is likely that the Dimasa Kacharis would have been more economically developed.

Table 3: Showing the traditional Dimasa Kachari opinion on the question of being more economically developed if sacrifices were not necessary

Different opinions	**Respondents**	**Percentage**
Will be more economically developed	39	55.71%
Will not be more economically developed	24	34.28%
Having no opinion	07	10.00%
Total	**70**	**100%**

The above table shows that 55.71% of the traditional Dimasa Kacharis expressed that the Dimasa Kacharis would be more economically developed if the sacrifices were not necessary, while 34.28% feel that they would not be more economically developed even if sacrifices were not necessary. There are 10.00% of respondents who have not shown their opinion. This table affirms that the sacrifices of the traditional Dimasa Kacharis are expensive and that if sacrifices were not necessary, then they would have been more economically developed.

The sacrifices as causal factors of poverty among the traditional Dimasa Kacharis may be further affirmed as follows. Firstly, almost all these sacrifices require livestock. While many Dimasa families rear livestock for consumption as well as commercial purposes; it will be extremely difficult for families who are working hard to make ends meet, to provide the huge amount of livestock demanded by these curative sacrifices. Therefore, once their own livestock has been exhausted, they have no other option but to buy the required animals which will cost a huge amount of money. Moreover, when the livestock that they rear for consumption as well as economic purposes are all used up for the performance of sacrifices, naturally it will have an adverse impact on their economic condition.

Secondly, if the sick person does not recover, the cycle of sacrifices goes on and on until the family becomes financially, mentally and physically drained. Since, it is the strong belief of the Dimasa Kacharis that once a sickness has been diagnosed and the malevolent spirit causing it has been identified, then the sacrifice must be done at all cost, or else it is unfavorable for the family. Therefore, there have been numerous cases of families that have attempted to perform the required sacrifices even by borrowing money from their relatives or neighbors.[176]

Thirdly, when sacrifices are offered at home it may be attended by a selected few men invited by the householder. These invitees are entertained with the consecrated meat. But, when the sacrifice is performed in the forest, any number of men can attend the worship and they would be entertained with the consecrated food. Entertaining the large number of participants even once would be a difficult task due to the involvement of not only meat, but other food items also. If the sacrifices are to be repeated again and again, it would be extremely strenuous for anyone to entertain the participants every time.

Fourthly, although K. Daulagupu asserts that the priest is not to demand any money for his service, the sacrificers are free to offer a fee as they deem fit as a token of gratitude.[177] But, Sarda Hojai asserts that there are some *Hojais* who demand a hefty sum of Rs. 4000-5000 per sacrifice.[178]

From the above table 80.00% of the respondents affirm that fees are given to the priest, while 10.00% responded by saying that they do not give any fees. There are 10.00% who have not shown their opinion. Thus, large amounts of money are exacted for the performance of a single sacrifice. A family may be able to afford a single sacrifice. But if the sacrifices go on and on, it will be extremely

[176] Tarzen Langthasa, Interview...

[177] Daulagupu, Interview...

[178] Sarda Hojai, Interview...

difficult for families to pay the *Hojai* his fees for each sacrifice performed.

Table 4: Showing the traditional Dimasa Kachari practice on the question whether or not the *Hojai/Phatri* is given fees

Different practices	Respondents	Percentage
Gives fees	56	80.00%
Does not give fees	07	10.00%
Having no opinion	07	10.00%
Total	**70**	**100%**

Furthermore, Lalronghaka Ngamlai emphasizes that, *Zu* being a necessity in every sacrifice, it is very expensive. During the celebration of *Busu*, the villagers compete among themselves to brew the sweetest and largest quantity of *Zu*.[179] Ramdina Lalsim also affirms that on the occasions of the community sacrifices, to brew *Zu*, the best quality rice is required which is very expensive.[180] This also has a severe impact on their economy. Moreover, scholars like Danda and Bordoloi have also asserted that during the celebration of *Busu*, well-to-do families have a tendency to spend about half of their annual production of food in entertaining friends and family.[181]

Table 5: Showing the Traditional Dimasa Kachari Opinion on the question of their willingness/unwillingness to stop offering sacrifices and their reasons

Different opinions	Respondents	Percentage	Reasons
Willing to stop sacrifice	21	30.00%	Due to its expensiveness
Unwilling to stop sacrifice	37	52.85%	No reason is mentioned
Having no opinion	12	17.14%	Nil
Total	**70**	**100%**	

[179] Ngamlai, Interview…

[180] Interview with Ramdina Lalsim, Writer and Historian, resident of Haflong, 19 November 2013. Hereafter cited as Lalsim, Interview…

[181] Bordoloi, *The Dimasa Kacharis…*; Danda, *Among the Dimasa…*

In spite of the sacrifices being causal factors of poverty, this table shows that only 30.00% of traditional Dimasa Kachari respondents expressed their willingness to stop offering sacrifices due to its expensiveness, whereas 52.85% are willing to continue although they have not mentioned as to why they want to continue offering sacrifice. There are 17.14% of respondents who have no opinion. Although no reason has been given, it seems that the traditional Dimasa Kacharis are unwilling to stop offering sacrifices due to a deep sense of loyalty towards their traditional religion. This is affirmed further by the next table which shows the opinion regarding the purpose of sacrifice in the traditional Dimasa Kachari religion.

Table 6: Showing the Traditional Dimasa Kachari opinion on the purpose of sacrifice in the traditional Dimasa Kachari religion

Different opinions	Respondents	Percentage
Strengthens the spiritual life	11	15.71%
Brings earthly blessings	10	14.28%
Is the religious foundation	27	38.57%
An unnecessary burden no effect on spiritual life	22	31.42%
Total	**70**	**100%**

The above table shows that 15.71% of respondents feel that sacrifice strengthens the spiritual life, while 14.28% feel that sacrifices bring earthly blessings and 38.57% feels that sacrifice is the religious foundation. There are 31.42% who feel that sacrifices are unnecessary burden with no spiritual implications. When the first three opinions are taken together, the percentage comes to 68.56%. Thus, one can affirm that the traditional Dimasa Kacharis value their sacrifices in spite of their expensiveness, and do not see it as unnecessary burden. Although, they feel that they would be more economically developed if sacrifices were not necessary, they are unwilling to stop offering sacrifices because the sacrifices strengthens their spiritual lives, brings earthly blessings and are the foundation of their traditional religion.

3. RELIGIOUS IMPACTS

It would be unmanageable to speak of worship as an unconnected component in the traditional Dimasa Kachari religion because it is intricately connected with their sacrifices. The New Lexicon Webster's Dictionary of the English Language defines 'worship' as, "reverence, homage or honour paid to God, ceremonies or services expressing such reverence."[182] In the traditional Dimasa Kachari religion, reverence and homage is paid to the benevolent deities through the sacrificial offerings of blood, meat *Zu,* etc. Hence, sacrificial worship occupies a big space in traditional Dimasa Kachari religion. Therefore, worship and sacrifice in the traditional Dimasa Kachari religion are intricately connected.

Thus, there are certain important religious impacts of sacrifice which may be enumerated as follows:

i) Communion between Worshippers and Worshipped

William Robertson Smith suggested that sacrifice was a way of creating communion between the worshippers and the divine entity being worshipped through the sharing of the sacrificial meal.[183]

Communion in the sense of a bond between the worshipper and the sacred power is fundamental to all sacrifice. Certain sacrifices, however, promote this communion by means of a sacramental meal. The meal may be one in which the sacrificial oblation is simply shared by the deity and the worshippers.[184]

The traditional Dimasa Kachari sacrifice usually consists of a sacramental meal in which the flesh of the sacrificial animal is shared by the members of the family, the clan or the village community. During the celebration of *Misengba,* the sacrificial meat is distributed among the people by the priest as divine favour (*misu*). Moreover, during the celebration of the grandest form of *Busu,* i.e., *Hangseu*

---

[182] "Worship," *The New Lexicon Webster's Dictionary of the English Language* (New York: Lexicon Publications Inc., 1988), 1135.

[183] Brenda Ralph Lewis, *Ritual Sacrifice: A Concise History* (England: Sutton Publishing Limited, 2001), 10.

[184] *The New Encyclopaedia Britannica,* 1981 ed., vol. 16, s.v; "Sacrifice", 128-135.

Manaoba, the village elders partake of the sacrificial meat with *Zu*. In this meal which is called *midogarba,* the youths and the children are prohibited from taking part.

Therefore, one can assume that the sacrifices of the traditional Dimasa Kacharis has a profound religious significance and impact as it makes the worshipper and the worshipped communicate and form a special bond of kinship. When looked in this way, sacrifice, as proclaimed by Durkheim, takes on a unique characteristic by playing the form of an "alimentary communion"[185] between the worshippers and the worshipped. The act of sacrifice acquires more virtue than a mere gift as it binds the worshippers and the worshipped together through the exchange of cordiality.[186]

ii) Providing Occasions for Community Worship

Sacrifice and the motive of offering sacrifice have been understood in various ways. But for W. Robertson Smith, the original motive of sacrifice is, "an effort at communion among the members of the group, on the other hand between them and their god."[187] Through the communion of the flesh and the blood of the sacrificed animal, the sacred and the profane realms were brought together. Thus the people united among themselves, could commune with god by sharing the food and the drink, in which god was believed immanent.[188]

Even though there is little scope of worshipping as a community on a routine basis, the traditional Dimasa Kacharis conduct community worship on specific occasions. During the observance of *Misengba* or *Busu*, it is mandatory for all the traditional Dimasa Kacharis to participate. On other occasions members of a particular village or a particular clan gather together and worship their respective deities. Hence, the community sacrifices unite the people and provide them occasions to worship as a community.

---

[185] Durkheim, *Elementary Forms...*, 337.

[186] C. Walu Walling, *Sacrifice and Salvation in Ao-Naga Tradition: A Theological Perspective* (Impur Nagaland: C. Walu Walling, 1997), 86.

[187] William A. Lessa and Evon Z. Vogt, eds., *Reader in Comparative Religion: An Anthropological Approach* (New York: Harper and Row, 1965), 39.

[188] Jose Thachil, *The Vedic and the Christian Concept of Sacrifice* (Kerala: The Pontifical Institute of Theology and Philosophy, 1985), 7.

Table 7: Showing the traditional Dimasa Kachari opinion on whether sacrifices provide occasions for community worship or not

Different opinions	Respondents	Percentage
Provides occasions	33	47.14%
Do not provide occasions	24	34.28%
Having no opinion	13	18. 57%
Total	**70**	**100%**

The above table clearly shows that 47.14% of the traditional Dimasa Kachari respondents express that the sacrifices provides occasions for community worship, while 34.28% do not think so and 18.57% do not have any opinion. Hence, the opinion of the majority shows that the traditional sacrifices of the Dimasa Kacharis has a profound religious impact by providing the people occasions to worship as a community and binds them together into a single moral community. These community sacrifices where the people participate for the welfare of the entire community are occasions for collective action binding the community members together in their beliefs.

iii) Providing Unity and Identity to the Community

The community sacrifices along with the traditional festivals demand the traditional Dimasa Kacharis to do away with all enmities and misunderstandings. Community sacrifices such as *Misengba* requires all the traditional Dimasa Kacharis to gather together for a common socio-religious cause and purpose as being members of the community and religion.

On other occasions such as *Krongfanggarba, Maisalaigarba,* etc., the community of a particular Dimasa Kachari village or their representatives attend the sacrifice offered for the general welfare and prosperity of the village community. During the *Sengphong Nimadai* sacrifice, all the clan members are also expected to take an active part.

Moreover, Lalronghaka Ngamlai also asserts that, the sacrifices unite the community, since the oracles of the priest must be obeyed by all the community members at any cost and disobedience may result in divine displeasure and punishment.[189] Furthermore, in these various community sacrifices, the sacrificial animals, cereals, etc., and all other expenses are borne by the community willingly. All these are jointly playing an important dynamic role as the kernel of their religious identity and providing unity to the people.

The three tables given below have been presented together to show the important role played by the sacrifices as uniting factor of the community members in order to preserve their identity and strengthen their traditional religion. The first table displays the traditional Dimasa Kachari opinion regarding the role of sacrifices in uniting the Dimasa Kachari community. The second table shows the traditional Dimasa Kachari opinion regarding the role of sacrifices in maintaining their traditional religion and the third table shows the opinion regarding the value of their traditional festivals. However, the evaluation of these three tables will be given collectively.

Table 8: Showing the traditional Dimasa Kachari opinion of whether or not sacrifices unite the whole village and the Dimasa community as a whole

Different opinions	**Respondents**	**Percentage**
Unites	31	44.28%
Does not unite	27	38.57%
Having no opinion	12	17.14%
Total	**70**	**100%**

Table 9: Showing the traditional Dimasa Kachari opinion on the question of sacrifices helping in the maintenance of Dimasa Kachari traditional religion

Different opinions	**Respondents**	**Percentage**
Has helped in maintenance	33	47.14 %
Has not helped	29	41.42 %
Having no opinion	18	11.42 %
Total	**70**	**100 %**

[189] Ngamlai, Interview…

Table 10: Showing the Traditional Dimasa Kachari opinion regarding the value of their traditional festivals

Different opinions	Respondents	Percentage
Value them very much	64	91.42%
Simply participate, never think of value	06	08.57%
Feel that they are a burden	00	00.00%
Total	**70**	**100%**

From the above three tables, we can clearly see that 44.28% of the respondents feel that the sacrifices have helped to unify the traditional Dimasa Kacharis and to affirm their identity. The second table shows that 47.14% of the respondents feel that the sacrifices have helped them to hold firmly their traditional religion and its implied practices. With regards to the importance of festivals, the third table shows that 91.42% value their traditional festivals very much.

Thus, the findings of questionnaire answers affirm that the traditional sacrifices have helped the traditional Dimasa Kacharis to be united and they have contributed a great value for the practitioners and it is these sacrifices that constitute valuable forms and elements of their religion. The togetherness of the traditional Dimasa Kacharis on occasions of community sacrifices helps them to be conscious of their oneness and unity as members of the same community with a particular ethnicity and religious identity. The sacrifices are the kernel of the Dimasa Kachari religious identity and have helped in the maintenance and survival of the traditional Dimasa Kachari religion

iv) Preservation of the Traditional Religious Functionaries

In almost all the tribal societies, there are specific religious functionaries who have either inherited their position from their foreparents, or they are elected as religious functionaries. They are called by different names in different tribes. The main function of these religious functionaries is to offer sacrifices at all the tribal festivals and other important occasions in social and individual life. They are in charge of keeping all the tribal deities happy and joyful.[190]

[190] Christopher Augustus Bixel Tirkey, *Religion/Primal Religions* (Delhi: ISPCK, 1998), 204.

The traditional Dimasa Kachari practice of sacrifices, being one of the factors constituting an integrated religious identity requires the presence of special people, such as *Gisia*, *Zonthais*, *Dainya* and *Baroa*, *Hojai* and *Phatri* to serve for the well-being and prosperity of the traditional Dimasa Kacharis.

Sacrifices during *Misengba* require the presence of the highest priest the *Gisia*, the *Zonthais*, the *Dainya and Baroa* to offer the sacrifices on behalf of the entire Dimasa Kachari community. In the village as well as most of the family rituals, the *Hojai* performs sacrifice and offers thanksgiving, prayers and petitions on behalf of the family or the village community. The divine will is conveyed to the people through the *Phatri*.

These religious specialists and functionaries hold a very important place in the religious system of the traditional Dimasa Kacharis and they are much feared and respected by the people because of their religious knowledge and special functions. They act as intermediaries between the deities and the people. They take care of the total well-being of the people by worshipping the deities. They are the core of the traditional beliefs and practices. The practice of offering sacrifices has helped in preserving the offices of these religious specialists. These religious functionaries in turn have helped in maintaining the age-old traditional beliefs and practices of the Dimasa Kacharis and the Dimasa Kacharis of today can learn their religious, cultural and traditional heritages from these religious specialists.

v) Preservation of Traditional Arts and Dresses

India is marked by its rich traditional heritage of tribal arts and culture. Since the days of remote past, the diversified art and cultural forms generated by the tribal and rural people of India have continued to show their creative magnificence. According to Vidyarthi and Rai, tribal art and crafts correspond to three types:[191]

a) *Ritualistic*: It is used in the service of rites associated with some beliefs and mystical ideas, viz., some stone, small hut, poles.

[191] L.P. Vidyarthi and Binay Kumar Rai, *The Tribal Culture of India* (New Delhi: Concept Publishing Company, 1976), 336.

b) *Utilitarian*: Social customs demand the object while modes of manufacture and material qualities determine the form. For example, basketry, pottery, carpet-making, garment-making, etc.
c) *Individualistic*: It expresses the feelings and emotions of the crafts experts, viz., weaving clothes, preparing a mat, etc.

Tribal art and religion fuse together with each other into a unified whole. Tribal art and crafts are mainly dominated and shaped by religious motifs, this relation between art and religion is a universal feature. They play an indispensable role in the worship of the deities. Tribal art and craft has religious connotation and a distinctive function, that is, the assertion of an identity. Through the paintings, crafts, songs and dances and traditional dresses, the community continues and preserves the rich traditional heritage of their ancestors. Thus, they are the expressions of an identity consciousness.

The traditional Dimasa Kacharis are a culturally rich tribe and the architectural remains clearly bear witness to this. The highly decorative designs of the cloths woven, the ornamental mats and other artistic handicrafts clearly show their skill and love for artistic designs. During *Busu*, as a mark of festivities and reception, the artistic ceremonial gate called *Fangsla* is constructed by the youths at the entrance of the village.

Furthermore, during the offering of sacrifices, instead of company made instruments and apparatus, locally made bamboo baskets, gourd pots and small clay figurines are utilized for carrying sacrificial items to the objects of their worship. The utilization of indigenous crafts and products exhibit the artistic skill of the Dimasa Kacharis.[192]

[192] The significance of the *Fangsla* and the use of clay figurines in the sacrifices have been described in Chapter Two Section 4 (iii) and Chapter Three Section 2 (v) (d).

The Dimasa Kacharis have a few musical instruments such as *Muree,*[193] *Muree-Wathesa,*[194] *Shupin,*[195] a string instrument called *Khram Dubong*[196] and a drum called *Khram.*[197] During the performance of any traditional dance, these musical instruments play an indispensable part. The skill of *Muree* playing is not known to everyone and those who know this art are called *Muree Damyaba.*[198] The traditional Dimasa Kacharis also have several dances that are performed mainly during the celebration of *Busu.* Among the traditional dances, *Madaikhilimba* is performed to pay homage to the deities. Here, mention may be made of the dance performed by the *Phatri.* It is believed that he gains divine power after dancing unceasingly for a long period. This dance must be accompanied with the music of the *Khram* and the *Muree.* Among the socio-religious festivals of the traditional Dimasa Kacharis, *Busu* being the gayest and most important community festival, singing and dancing is an important element of the festivities. The unceasing sound of the *Khrams* and the *Muree* is accompanied by dancing, feasting and drinking.

The traditional dresses of the Dimasa Kacharis are colourful and beautiful. The dresses of the Dimasa Kacharis have been much influenced by westernization with Dimasa Kacharis wearing western dresses in their daily day-to-day lives. However, community sacrifices and festivals require the community members to put on their best traditional dresses and ornaments to take part in the festivities. During the performance of sacrifices, the priest is required to wear the traditional turban and loincloth called *Rithar.* Moreover, traditional clothes are also given as gifts to the priests.

---

[193] It is a long wooden pipe consisting of three pieces and its length is about 1.75 metres. It is indispensable in every dance.

[194] It is a smaller *Muree* or trumpet produced from a special kind of bamboo tube.

[195] It is a kind of flute made of a small thin bamboo.

[196] It is somewhat like the Jewish harp and made from the reeds of the *dubong,* a kind of grass.

[197] It is a wooden drum measuring about 1.25 metres.

[198] They are the traditional musicians skilled in the art of playing the *Muree.*

Table 11: Showing the traditional Dimasa Kachari opinion on the question of the Dimasa Kachari traditional dress

Different opinions	Respondents	Percentage
Appreciate very much	69	98.57%
Do not appreciate	01	01.42%
Having no opinion	00	00.00%
Total	**70**	**100%**

The above table clearly shows that 98.57% of the traditional Dimasa Kacharis appreciate and value their traditional dress very much while only 01.42% does not appreciate. Therefore, taking into consideration the opinion of the majority, one can affirm that the traditional Dimasa Kacharis have a deep value and appreciation for their traditional dresses, art and crafts.

The impact of traditional sacrifices of the Dimasa Kacharis can be felt in the sphere of preservation of their traditional crafts, musical instruments, the special musicians called *Muree Damyaba*, traditional dresses and their colourful dances. It is during the celebration of the community sacrifices that one can see the traditional Dimasa Kachari arts and crafts in all its beauty. Ramdina Lalsim also affirms that since the traditional musical instruments are intricately connected with their religious rituals, the sacrifices play an important role in the preservation of the culture, traditions, music and art of the Dimasa Kacharis.[199] Thus, if not for the observance of the various sacrifices all these traditional art forms would have been lost in time or many of them would be museum pieces.

4. CONCLUDING REMARKS

From the above discussion one can conclude by saying that the sacrifices of the traditional Dimasa Kacharis has profound impacts upon the socio-economic and religious life of the practitioners. The sacrifices teaches the people valuable socio-ethical values related to respect for the elders, respect for the land and to live their religion through their practical day-to-day lives. The sacrifices, demanding the active participation of every individual and every family has

[199] Lalsim, Interview...

significance for social cohesion and unity. Community sacrifices provides the people occasions to worship together as a community with a specific ethnicity and religious identity and binds them together into a single moral community. Moreover, they play an important role in the preservation of the traditional religious specialists and functionaries as well as the traditional art forms such as dances, dresses, musical instruments and players, and crafts.

However, these sacrifices have also certain negative impacts due to their expensiveness and the rampant use of rice beer. Nevertheless, the traditional Dimasa Kacharis are unwilling to give up their sacrifices as they are the constitutive parts and elements of their religion and the core of their religious identity and their religious foundation.

Chapter 5

CONCLUSION

The discussion on the impact of sacrifices upon the socio-economic and religious life of the traditional Dimasa Kacharis although incomplete needs to be concluded due to the constraint of time and space. However, from what has been discussed, one can discern that the sacrifices have deep socio-economic and religious impacts and value for the practitioners and it is the kernel of their religious and ethnic identity.

In spite of the negative impacts upon their socio-economic lives, the traditional Dimasa Kacharis are unwilling to stop offering sacrifices. Moreover, any effort to put a stop to the practice of offering sacrifices may provoke protests from the community as intrusion upon their religious rites. Hence, in conclusion certain measures that do not infringe upon the traditional Dimasa Kacharis may be proposed as prospects and challenges to thwart the negative impact of sacrifice.

In order to negate the negative impacts of sacrifice upon the socio-economic and religious life of the traditional Dimasa Kacharis, **the rich tribal heritage and moral ethics must be revived, reinterpreted and rediscovered by the Dimasa Kacharis**. For this, Dimasa Kachari religious leaders, social leaders and youth leaders must play an active role. The senior citizens of the community must endeavor to impart the valuable cultural heritage and moral ethics to the younger generation orally as well as through print media.

In reviving and reinterpreting the tribal heritage, firstly, **the Dimasa Kachari concept of land must be rediscovered**. For the traditional Dimasa Kacharis, land is owned by the community and it is not only the source of their livelihood but, also the source of their culture, religion and history. The land is their ancestral property, a gift from *Madai.*[200] Therefore, the traditional Dimasa Kacharis cannot think of commercialization of land to earn wealth. They are satisfied by what the land produces for them. Any surplus produce is shared with among the community members and if they need anything they exchange for it. Excess wealth is considered to be the source of enmity and bitterness. Therefore, this socio-cultural heritage of sharing the produce of the land must be rediscovered and revived among the traditional Dimasa Kacharis of today.

Secondly, **the principles and values of the traditional youth institution (*Hangseu*) which includes both boys and girls must be revived and treasured**. *Hangseu* is an economic institution based on the principles of co-operation and mutual help. Any family unable to work by themselves may engage the youths to work in their fields for a nominal charge. The payment can be made by the family after the harvest and this collection made by the *Hangseu* is spent collectively in the celebration of *Busu*. Hence, this institution that has been helping the poor, the sick, the widows and other needy persons of the village must be revived and treasured by the present-day Dimasa Kacharis.

Thirdly, **the traditional Dimasa Kachari clan system must be reinterpreted to be more holistic**. As has been mentioned earlier, the clan system among the Dimasa Kacharis is so strong that fulfillment of clan obligations is a must. Each member of the clan

---

[200] The land is the source of livelihood for the traditional Dimasa Kacharis. It is the land that provides them their everyday needs. The land also provides them with their religious needs. It is from the land that the Dimasa Kacharis procure the materials necessary for their sacrifices. The people, even though they do not know the habitation of *Madai*, the Supreme Creator, they experience his continuous presence in their midst in the nature and natural objects. Hence, land is the gift of *Madai* to the Dimasa Kacharis.

has the responsibility to provide help to the poor, widows and needy persons of the clan. This socio-cultural heritage of helping poor and needy members of one's clan must be rediscovered and modified to extend even outside the clan system.

Another prospect that may be suggested is the **promotion of ethno-medicinal system**. A study done by P. Tamuli and P. Sharma has brought to light folklore medicinal uses of 25 plant species among the Dimasa Kacharis.[201] Meanwhile, a study done by J. Rout, A. Sajem and M. Nath has identified 47 plant species used by the traditional Dimasa Kacharis for the treatment of various diseases.[202] This medicinal system has been transmitted orally through the generations and no written records are available till today. The Dimasa people should be encouraged to preserve this distinctive cultural heritage and to resort to these medicinal plants instead of offering expensive sacrifices. Furthermore, the Government must also take steps for the development of these traditional methods and the conservation of these medicinal plants that are fast disappearing due to deforestation and wanton destruction of the ecology.

Another measure that may also be suggested is the **provision of better healthcare facilities by the government.** From the questionnaire to the traditional Dimasa Kacharis, 52.85% responded that they are not satisfied with the healthcare facilities provided by the government in their village, whereas 41.42% are quite satisfied. There are 05.71% who did not express any opinion.[203]

The opinion of the majority questionnaire respondents affirm that the healthcare facilities provided by the government in Dima Hasao district are very much inadequate. There are a total number

---

[201] P. Tamuli and P. Sharma, "Ethno-medico-botany of the Dimasa Kachari of North Cachar Hills district of Assam," *Indian Journal of Traditional Knowledge* 9/4 (October, 2010): 720.

[202] Jayashree Rout, Albert L. Sajem and Minaram Nath, "Medicinal plants of North Cachar Hills district of Assam used by the Dimasa tribe," *Indian Journal of Traditional Knowledge* 11/3 (July, 2012): 520.

[203] Findings from Answers to Q, No. 33 of Questionnaire to traditional Dimasa Kacharis.

of 539 villages in Dima Hasao district,[204] and as per the record of the Joint Director, Health Services, Dima Hasao, Assam, the various healthcare facilities available in Dima Hasao are as follows: Civil Hospital – 01; Rural Hospitals – 02; PHC – 03; Mini PHC – 02; Subsidiary Health Centres – 02; State Dispensaries – 02; Family Welfare Sub-Centres – 58.[205]

Therefore, the onus is on the government to take steps and provide better healthcare facilities to the people so that they do not have to resort to expensive sacrifices for their treatment. As of now, since the government is unable to meet all the demands of the public in matters of healthcare facilities, the ethno-medicinal system of the traditional Dimasa Kacharis is still a viable option that needs to be preserved and developed.

Still another measure that may be suggested is the **provision of better educational facilities by the government**. G.C. Pande asserts that, "…impact of education on attitudes is well known. It creates a philosophical vaccum [sic] and search for a new horizon."[206] Among the traditional Dimasa Kacharis and the Christian Dimasa Kacharis, 94.28% and 55.55% respectively feel that education is the means of development for the entire Dimasa Kachari community. On the other hand, 05.71% and 38.88% respectively feel that education alone would not suffice.[207]

Hence, going with the majority opinion, we can affirm that education is the means through which the Dimasa Kachari community may be more developed. However, education alone is not enough for development. But through education the people can be enlightened to comprehend and thereby enabled to understand the negative impacts of their traditional sacrifices and search for a new horizon.

---

204 "Administration," http://nchills.gov.in/NCHILLS-ADMIN.htm (26 January 2014).

205 Joint Director, Health Services, Dima Hasao, Assam, *Statistical Report for the year 2012*, 2012.

206 G.C. Pande, *Indian Tribes The Habitat, Society, Economy and Change* (New Delhi: Anmol Publications, 1991), 53.

207 Findings from Answers to Q. No. 30 of Questionnaire to traditional Dimasa Kacharis and Q. No. 12 of Questionnaire to Christian Dimasa Kacharis.

In this regard, the government has a definite role to play by providing better educational facilities to the people. At present, the educational facilities available in Dima Hasao district is as follows: Colleges – 03; Higher Secondary – 09; High Schools – 87; Middle Schools – 178; Lower Primary Schools – 750; Adult Education – 01; Technical – 01; Junior Colleges – 03.[208]

However, there is also a detrimental facet of the impact of education on tribals which must be taken into account and dealt with. This aspect seen among educated tribal youths is the love of town life only and the unwillingness to return to the village life or even to work for the welfare of their people. This is also one of the reasons for the decline of cultural heritage among the traditional Dimasa Kacharis.

Therefore, in promoting education among the Dimasa Kacharis, they must be educated for maturity to understand the positive as well as negative aspects of tribal society. In this way they can preserve their unique tribal heritages and their identity, "…when they have rediscovered their selfhood, they will begin to love all that is good in tribal society."[209]

Even though it is acknowledged that this research does not intend to discuss mission strategy among the Dimasa Kacharis, **a missiological challenge** arises out of the analysis of the various impacts of sacrifice on the life of the traditional Dimasa Kacharis.

Bordoloi has asserted that, "…all attempts on the part of the Christian Missionaries to convert them (the Dimasa Kacharis) into Christianity have proved to be futile."[210] This is true to a certain degree because even after many years of mission work among the Dimasa Kacharis, there are only a handful of Christian Dimasa Kacharis in Dima Hasao district.[211] It is possible that Christianity

---

[208] Inspector of Schools, Dima Hasao district, Assam. *Statistical Report for the year 2013*, 2013.

[209] M.M. Thomas and R.W. Taylor, eds., *Tribal Awakening: A Group Study* (Bangalore: Christian Institute for the Study of Religion and Society, 1965), 66.

[210] Bordoloi, *The Dimasa Kacharis…*, 76.

[211] Even though there is no official statistical report, there are reportedly around 200-250 Christian Dimasa Kacharis in the entire Dima Hasao district. Phonendra Naiding, Interview…

has not been presented in a way that is attractive for the Dimasa Kacharis. Therefore, if a paradigm shift is not brought about in the missiological strategy adopted by the Church it could be extremely difficult to bring the entire Dimasa Kachari community under the fold of Christianity.

From the questionnaire distributed among Christian Dimasa Kacharis in Dima Hasao, 100% of questionnaire respondents conveyed that Dimasa Kacharis would be developed if they embrace Christianity.[212] Christian leaders working among the Dimasa Kacharis are also of the opinion that Christianity would make the Dimasa Kacharis more developed. However, they expressed the need of contextualizing and indigenizing traditional Dimasa Kachari culture and values into Christianity, as well as the need of more native workers.[213] Furthermore, 72.22% of the Christian Dimasa Kachari respondents expressed that they are not satisfied with the work of the Church among the Dimasa Kacharis, while 27.77% expressed their satisfaction.[214]

Contextualizing and indigenizing the traditional Dimasa Kachari values and principles seem to be a viable missiological strategy due to the various misinterpretations and misrepresentations of Christianity among the traditional Dimasa Kacharis.[215]

---

[212] Findings from Answers to Q. No. 13 of Questionnaire to Christian Dimasa Kacharis.

[213] Interview with Insaan Johori, Evangelist, resident of N.D. Razi, Haflong, 14 November 2013; Interview with Mondol Langthasa, Evangelist, resident of Haflong, 17 November 2013. Interview with V.L. Tluanga Bapui, Convenor, Dimasa Kachari Bible Translation, resident of Mission Compound, Haflong, 15 November 2013. Hereafter cited as Bapui, Interview…

[214] Findings from Answers to Q. No. 16 of Questionnaire to Christian Dimasa Kacharis.

[215] Some of the thoughts of traditional Dimasa Kacharis towards Christianity and Christians are, Christianity is the religion of the Hmar, Kuki, Naga and other tribes. To become a Christian means to lose one's culture and traditions. During the time of baptism, one has to drink the urine of a cow. The Christian Dimasa Kacharis are *gusu* (impure) as they eat cow's meat. Since they are impure, Christian Dimasa Kacharis do not have the right to wear their traditional dresses or celebrate their traditional social festivals. Joton Hojai, Interview…

The tribals practice ethical and moral values and severe measures are arranged to deal with the ethical moral problems within the community, these are primarily in the form of oral traditions handed down from generation to generation. The richness of tribal oral tradition has been beautifully described by Renthy Keitzer, who calls it the unwritten "Prime Bible" by writing the following words:

> These (oral traditions) may be called as the unwritten 'Prime Bible' of the tribal/indigenous people. One can find in these oral traditions their beliefs, norms, and practices; hence a great and rich treasure of theological value is hidden with this 'Prime Bible' of the people.[216]

The traditional Dimasa Kachari observance of various taboos may also be conveniently utilized, as taboo plays an important role in the social cohesion of the people. Taboos also serve as a positive purpose for focusing one's life on the divine and the purposes of the divine.[217] The observance of many taboos related to hunting, fishing and cutting of trees, etc., may also be utilized to enhance sensitivity towards the eco-system and to discourage the people from sacrificing many innocent animals.

The traditional Dimasa Kacharis usually cremate the corpse. However, people dying unnatural deaths cannot be cremated but to be buried.[218] It seems that due to this practice, many traditional Dimasa Kacharis abhor the idea of being buried if they become Christians. Therefore, the Church would do well to contemplate on giving a choice or option either to cremate or bury the corpses of Dimasa Kacharis who become Christians.[219]

---

[216] Renthy Keitzer, *In Search of a Relevant Gospel Message* (Guwahati: CLC, 1995), 85.

[217] Kechutzar, *Rethinking...*, 181.

[218] If a person dies after being attacked by a tiger, it is considered most unfortunate and the dead body cannot be cremated. The dead body is buried outside the village boundary by the clan members. Death from leprosy, black fever and cholera are also regarded as unfortunate deaths and the victims are not cremated but buried.

[219] Bapui, Interview...

Moreover, the development of a relevant contextual theology is also the need of the hour for an effective Christian mission among the Dimasa Kacharis. In this regard, the Church could follow the approach of contextualisation and indigenisation represented by senior thinkers like Nirmal Minz and the late Renthy Keitzer who suggests for adaptation of the tribal cultural values.[220]

In order to develop a contextual theology to negate the negative impacts of sacrifice, the Church should inculcate the ethical and religious values of the traditional Dimasa Kacharis. For example, for the traditional Dimasa Kacharis, the blood of the sacrificial victim is pure and holy and has the power to purify from every impurity and also to purify the land to become productive. For this reason, blood is mixed with water to make holy-water or *dithar*. This aspect of sacrifice may be interpreted to reiterate the efficacy of Christ's blood for the purification and remission of sins and how the salvific work of Christ has the power to bring holistic healing to everyone.

Additionally, the Dimasa Kachari belief in the existence of numerous malevolent spirits who can harm human beings is the main reason why sacrifices have to be offered to appease them. But, the benevolent ancestral deity *Sibrai* seems to be more powerful than all these malevolent spirits because it was *Sibrai* who ordered them to dwell in the natural habitats such as rocks, trees, rivers etc.[221] However, he has nothing to do with the spiritual salvation of the people. In developing a contextual Christian theology, Christ may be interpreted as one who is more powerful than evil spirits and one who is feared by evil spirits. He may be inferred as the physical and spiritual Saviour of human beings from the attacks of evil spirits. A Saviour who does not need to be appeased by offering expensive sacrifices, but one who demands a spiritual sacrifice of the believer's life.

---

[220] K.P. Aleaz, "A Tribal Theology from a Tribal Worldview," *Indian Journal of Theology*, 44/1 & 2 (2002): 20.

[221] See Creation Narrative of the Dimasa Kacharis narrated in Chapter Two Section 5 (i)

Therefore, the Church in Dima Hasao district is challenged to put in more effort and bring about a paradigm shift in the ministry among the Dimasa Kacharis for a holistic ministry.

Finally, sacrifice in the traditional Dimasa Kachari religion has undoubtedly made deep-rooted impacts upon the socio-economic and religious life of the traditional Dimasa Kacharis. The importance of these various impacts necessitates an increased investigation to the implication of the sacrifices.

Throughout history, sacrifice has been of deep significance to individuals and social groups. For the traditional Dimasa Kacharis also, sacrifices demand obedience and co-operation of the entire community. It is the kernel of their religious identity and ethnicity by binding them together into a single moral community through their active participation as members of an ethnic community.

Therefore, sacrifice has a deep religious value for them. It is a symbolic act that establishes a vertical relationship between divine and human, and a horizontal relationship between a human and another fellow human. Therefore, sacrifices for the traditional Dimasa Kacharis are the very heart of their religious life.

APPENDICES

APPENDIX-I
QUESTIONNAIRE TO TRADITIONAL DIMASA KACHARIS

1. **What is your present source of livelihood?**
    a) *Jhum* (Shifting cultivation)
    b) Livestock
    c) Cottage Industry
    d) Other
2. **Do you want to take up any other occupation other than your present occupation?**
    a) Yes
    b) No
    c) I don't know
3. **What is your preference for permanent occupation?**
    a) *Jhum* (Shifting cultivation)
    b) Govt. service
    c) Daily labour under private employment
    d) Cottage industry, weaving etc.
4. **What meat do you like best for curry?**
    a) Pork
    b) Chicken

   c) Fish
   d) Buffalo

5. **From where do you get your favourite meat?**
   a) Market
   b) Private shop
   c) Jungle
   d) We rear by ourselves

6. **From where do you get cooking instruments such as pot, vessels, utensils etc.?**
   a) Market
   b) Private shop
   c) We make pottery by ourselves

7. **How do you make your traditional dress?**
   a) Our women weave and stitch our clothes
   b) We buy readymade clothes and stitch them
   c) We buy readymade garments from shops
   d) We get our clothes as gifts

8. **From where do you get most of the raw materials for weaving?**
   a) We grow by ourselves
   b) We get from shops
   c) We get them from others

9. **Do you appreciate your Dimasa traditional dress?**
   a) Yes
   b) No
   c) No idea

10. **How do you feel about your Dimasa religion?**
    a) I am quite satisfied
    b) I am not very satisfied
    c) I am so dissatisfied that I want to embrace other religion
    d) I simply follow, I never think seriously

11. **How do you reflect on your traditional festivals?**
    a) I value them very much
    b) I simply participate, I never think of their value
    c) I feel that they are a burden for me

12. Do you think festivals are related with religion?

a) They are only occasions of joy and merriment
b) They are required for the worship of deities
c) They are a burden but necessary for religion
d) Some are related with religion while some are not

13. Do you believe in the existence of benevolent spirits?

a) Yes
b) No
c) No idea

14. Do you believe in the existence of malevolent spirits?

a) Yes
b) No
c) No idea

15. Do you offer sacrifices to these spirits?

a) Yes
b) No
c) I don't know

16. To whom do you offer sacrifices more often?

a) Benevolent
b) Malevolent
c) Both equally

17. What do you offer to these spirits?

a) Livestock
b) Vegetables
c) Others (Please specify)

18. Were you successful in your purpose of offering sacrifice?

a) Yes
b) No
c) I don't know

19. Do you believe the benevolent deities will punish you if you do not offer sacrifices?

a) Yes
b) No
c) No idea

20. Do you believe the malevolent spirits will punish you if you do not offer sacrifices?
   a) Yes
   b) No
   c) No idea

21. What is the purpose of sacrifice in the traditional Dimasa religion?
   a) Sacrifice strengthens the spiritual life
   b) Sacrifice brings earthly blessings
   c) Sacrifice is the religious foundation
   d) Sacrifice is an unnecessary burden and expense that does not affect the spiritual life of the Dimasa Kacharis.

22. Do you want to stop offering sacrifices? If yes why?
   a) Yes
   b) No
   c) No idea

____

23. Do you think the Dimasa identity is dead if Dimasa religion and sacrifices are not maintained?
   a) Yes
   b) No
   c) No idea

24. Do you think the sacrifices provide occasions for community worship?
   a) Yes
   b) No
   c) No idea

25. Do you feel that the sacrificial rituals unite the whole village and the Dimasa community as a whole?
   a) Yes
   b) No
   c) No idea

26. Do you feel that sacrifices have helped in the maintenance of Dimasa traditional religion?
   a) Yes

b) No
c) No idea

27. Do you think that you can continue to practice your traditional religion without offering sacrifices?
a) Yes
b) No
c) No idea

28. Do you feel that the sacrifices are expensive?
a) Yes
b) No
c) No idea

29. If the sacrifices were not necessary, do you feel that you would be more economically developed?
a) Yes
b) No
c) No idea

30. Do you think that education is the means of development for the whole Dimasa community?
a) Yes
b) No
c) No idea

31. Are you happy/satisfied with the educational measures introduced in your village?
a) Yes
b) No
c) No idea

32. Which would you prefer for the treatment of sicknesses?
a) Sacrifices
b) Medical treatments
c) Both

33. Are you happy/satisfied with the health facilities provided in your village?
a) Yes
b) No
c) No idea

34. When you are sick to whom do you go?

a) Doctor
b) Healthworker
c) *Phatri*
d) *Hojai*

35. If you consult *Hojai/Phatri* do you give him something as fee?

a) Yes
b) No
c) I don't know

36. Do you think that the use of modern development facilities such as education, medicine, etc., will cause you to give up your Dimasa traditional religion?

a) Yes
b) No
c) No idea

37. Do you think that the Dimasa traditional religion is slowly reduced by mingling with other religions?

a) Yes
b) No
c) No idea

Particulars of respondents:

Age: **Sex:** **Village:**

Status in Dimasa society:

APPENDIX-II
QUESTIONNAIRE TO CHRISTIAN DIMASA KACHARIS

1. What is your means of livelihood?

a) *Jhum* cultivation
b) Rearing livestock
c) Govt. service
d) Cottage Industry
e) Others (Please specify)

2. What is your preference for permanent occupation?

a) *Jhum* cultivation
b) Govt. service
c) Daily labour under private employment
d) Cottage industry
e) Having a portion of land for permanent cultivation

3. Why did you convert to Christianity leaving your traditional Dimasa religion?

a) I was invited to become a Christian by Christian friends
b) I was deeply influenced by Christian teachings and principles
c) I feel that Christianity would help me in overall development
d) I was completely disillusioned and dissatisfied with my traditional religion

4. Are all members of your family Christians?

a) Yes
b) No

c) Half are Christians

5. **Are you trying to convert your non-Christian family members, friends and relatives to Christianity?**
   a) Yes, I am trying
   b) No, I am not trying

6. **After becoming a Christian have you offered sacrifice to the traditional spirits and deities?**
   a) Yes
   b) No

7. **What is the purpose of sacrifice in the traditional Dimasa religion?**
   a) Sacrifice strengthens the spiritual life
   b) Sacrifice brings earthly blessings
   c) Sacrifice is the religious foundation
   d) Sacrifice is unnecessary burden and expense that does not affect the spiritual life of the Dimasa Kacharis

8. **Do you think that sacrifices are necessary for the survival of traditional Dimasa Kachari religion?**
   a) Yes
   b) No
   c) No idea

9. **Are sacrifices successful in their purpose?**
   a) Yes
   b) No
   c) To some extent

10. **Do you think that the offering of sacrifices provide occasions to worship as a community?**
   a) Yes
   b) No
   c) No idea

11. **Do you think that the offering of sacrifices unites the whole Dimasa community?**
   a) Yes
   b) No
   c) No idea

12. **Do you think that education is the means of development for the whole Dimasa community?**
    a) Yes
    b) No
    c) No idea
13. **Do you think that Dimasas would be more developed if they embraced Christianity?**
    a) Yes
    b) No
    c) No idea
14. **How has your clan responded to your becoming a Christian?**
    a) I have been excommunicated
    b) I have been threatened with excommunication
    c) There has been no response.
15. **After becoming a Christian do you still feel united with non-Christian Dimasas?**
    a) Yes
    b) No
    c) No Idea
16. **Are you satisfied with the work of the Church among the Dimasa community?**
    a) Yes
    b) No
    c) No idea
17. **How would mission work among the Dimasa community be more effective?**

    ____

Particulars of the respondents:

Age: **Sex:**

Village: **Year of Conversion:**

APPENDIX-III
LIST OF PERSONS INTERVIEWED

Sl. No.	Name	Designation	Place	Date	Time
1.	Denon Naiding	Ordinary person	N.D. Razi	26.05.13	10:00-13:00 hrs
2.	Dr. V.L. Tluanga Bapui	Convenor, Dimasa Kachari Bible Translation	Mission Compound, Haflong	15.11.13	09:00-10:30 hrs
3.	Insaan Johori	Evangelist	N.D. Razi	14.11.13	07:00-08:30 hrs
4.	Joton Hojai	Ordinary Person	Boildhura	15.11.13	07:00-08:30 hrs
5.	K. Daulagupu	Hojai	Haflong	19.11.13	12:30-14:00 hrs
6.	Mondol Langthasa	Evangelist	Haflong	17.11.13	08:00-10:00 hrs
7.	Palon Ch. Warisa	Retired Govt. Servant	Sarkari Bagan	12.11.13	08:30-10:30 hrs.
8.	Phonendra Naiding	Ordinary person	Haflong	18.11.13	07:00-08:00 hrs
9.	Ramdina Lalsim	Writer, Historian	Haflong	19.11.13	15:00-17:00 hrs
10.	Rev. Lalronghaka Ngamlai	Ex-Evangelist, Minister	Haflong	18.11.13	18:30-20:30 hrs
11.	Sajal Bathari	Ordinary person	N.D. Razi	19.11.13	06:30-08:30 hrs
12.	Sarda Hojai	Former Hojai	Natun Wari	26.05.13	13:00-15:00 hrs
13.	Tarzen Langthasa	Ordinary person	N.D. Razi	26.05.13	10:00-13:00 hrs

SOURCES CONSULTED

Books and Periodicals

Aleaz, K.P. "A Tribal Theology from a Tribal Worldview." *Indian Journal of Theology*, 44/1&2 (2002): 20-29.

________ . *Dimensions of Indian Religion: Study, Experience and Interaction*. Calcutta: Punthi Pustak, 1995.

Barkataki, S. *Tribes of Assam.* New Delhi: National Book Trust, India, 1984.

Barpujari, S.K. *History of the Dimasa: From the Earliest times to 1896 A.D.* Haflong: R. Langthasa, Cultural and Publicity Officer, Autonomous Council, N.C. Hills (Assam), Haflong, 1997.

Barua, Suparna. "A Woman in Dimasa Society-A Note." In *Communities of North-East India: An Anthropological Perspective.* Edited by Farida Ahmed Das and Indira Barua. New Delhi: Mittal Publications, 1996.

Bordoloi, B.N. *The Dimasa Kacharis of Assam*. Guwahati: Tribal Research Institute, 1984.

Bordoloi, B.N., G.C. Sarma Thakur and M.C. Saikia. *Tribes of Assam Part I.* Guwahati: Tribal Research Institute, 1987.

Chatry, K.K. "Ecological Significance of the Traditional Beliefs and Practices of Dimasa Kachari Tribe. *Indian Journal of Theology* 43/1&2(2001): 63-67.

Chatterji, Saral K., ed. *Society and Culture in North-East India.* Delhi: ISPCK, 1996.

Choudhury, Kamal Narayan. *Folklore in North-Eastern India.* Calcutta: Punthi Pustak, 2001.

Danda, Dipali G. *Among the Dimasa of Assam: An Ethnographic Study.* New Delhi: Sterling Publishers Pvt. Ltd., 1978.

Das, S. T. *Life Style: Indian Tribes: Locational Practice, Vol. I.* Delhi: Gyan Publishing House, 1987.

Durkheim, Emile. "*The Elementary Forms of the Religious Life.*" Translated by Joseph Ward Swain. London: George Allen & Unwin Ltd., 1915.

Endle, Sidney. *The Kacharis.* Delhi: Cosmo Publications, 1975.

Gait, Edward. *A History of Assam.* 2nd ed. Guwahati: Lawyer's Book Stall, 1926.

Ghosh, G.K. *Tribals and their Culture in Assam, Meghalaya and Mizoram, Vol. 1.* New Delhi: Ashish Publishing House, 1992.

Hagzer, Nirupama. *Dimasa.* Jorhat: Asom Sahitya Sabha, 1974.

Howells, William. *The Heathens: Primitive Man and His Religions.* Salem, Wisconsin: Sheffield Publishing Company, 1986.

Karotemprel, Sebastian, ed. *The Tribes of Northeast India.* Shillong: Vendrame Missiological Institute, 1984.

Kechutzar, Sashikaba. "Rethinking Naga Religious Traditions: An Exploration of Tribal Christian Spirituality." In *Theologizing Tribal Heritage – A Critical Re-Look.* Edited by Hrangthan Chhungi. Delhi: CWM/ISET-ECC/PCI/ISPCK, 2008.

Keitzer, Renthy. *In Search of a Relevant Gospel Message.* Guwahati: CLC, 1995.

Kumar, B.B. *The Tribal Societies of India: A Macro Perception.* New Delhi: Omsons Publications, 1998.

Lalrinawma, V.S. *Mizo Ethos: Changes and Challenges.* Aizawl: Mizoram Publication Board, 2005.

Lalsim, Ramdina. *Tribes of N.C. Hills, Assam.* Haflong: Cultural & Publicity Officer, N.C. Hills Autonomous Council, Haflong, Assam, 2005.

Langthasa, Padmini. "Traditional Methods of Conflict Management among the Dimasa." In *Traditional Method of Conflict Resolution in Three Tribal Societies of North East India*. Edited by Alphonsus D'Souza. Guwahti: North Eastern Social Research Centre, 2011.

Lessa, William A. and Evon Z. Vogt, eds. *Reader in Comparative Religion: An Anthropological Approach*. New York: Harper and Row, 1965.

Lewis, Brenda Ralph. *Ritual Sacrifice: A Concise History.* England: Sutton Publishing Limited, 2001.

Longchar, A. Wati. *The Traditional Tribal Worldview and Modernity.* Jorhat: Eastern Theological College, 2000.

________ . *The Tribal Religious Traditions in North East India – An Introduction.* Jorhat: Eastern Theological College, 2000.

Lott, Eric J. "Approaching a Religious Tradition." In *Religious Traditions of India*. Edited by P.S. Daniel, David C. Scott and G. R. Singh. Delhi: ISPCK, 2002.

Mahapatra, Mary D. *Tribal Religion and Rituals: Accounts of Superstition, Sorcery and Spirits.* New Delhi: Dominant Publishers and Distributors, 2001.

Medhi, Pramod and Sachin Kumar Borthakur. "Sacred groves and sacred plants of the Dimasas of North Cachar Hills of Northeast India." *African Journal of Plant Science* 7/2, (February, 2013): 67-77.

Minz, Nirmal. "The Study of Tribal Religion in India." In *Re-visioning India's Religious Traditions: Essays in Honour of Eric Lott.* Edited by David C. Scott and Israel Selvanayagam. Delhi: ISPCK, 1996.

Morris, Brian. *Anthropological Studies of Religion: An Introductory Text.* USA: Cambridge University Press, 1987.

Nath, Tushar Kanti. *Dimasa Sanskritir Abhash*. Haflong: Bhasha Sanskriti Akademi Assam Haflong, Dima Hasao, 2006.

Pande, G.C. *Indian Tribes: The Habitat, Society, Economy and Change.* New Delhi: Anmol Publications, 1991.

Presler, H. H. *Primitive Religion in India*. Madras: CLS, 1971.

Pritchard, E.E. Evans. *Theories of Primitive Religion*. Oxford, London: Oxford University Press, 1965.

Rhodes, N. G. and S.K. Bose. *A History of the Dimasa Kacharis - As Seen through Coinage*. New Delhi : Mira Basu Publishers, 2006.

Robertson, Roland, ed. *Sociology of Religion: Selected Readings*. Australia: Penguin Books, 1969.

Robertson, S. *Approaching Religion in a Pluralistic Context*. Bangalore: BTESSC/SATHRI, 2010.

Rout, Jayashree, Albert L. Sajem and Minaram Nath. "Medicinal plants of North Cachar Hills district of Assam used by the Dimasa tribe." *Indian Journal of Traditional Knowledge* 11/3 (July, 2012): 520-527.

Roy, Babul and A.N.M. Irshad Ali. "Medical Pluralism and Acceptance of the Different Medical Options Among the Dimasa Kacharis of North Cachar Hills in Assam." *Journal of Human Ecology* 12/1 (2001): 25-32.

Roy, Babul. "Descent Groupings, Belief System and Social Structure among the Dimasa Kacharis of Assam." *Man in India* 82/1&2 (2002): 73-99.

Schneider, Louis. *Sociological Approach to Religion*. New York: John Wiley & Sons Inc., 1970.

Sengupta, S. "Kachari Dimasa." In *People of Assam Volume XV Part One*. Edited by K.S. Singh. Calcutta: Anthropological Survey of India, 2003.

Smart, Ninian. *The Religious Experience of Mankind*. 3rd ed. New York: Charles Scribner & Sons, 1984.

Soppit, C. A. *Historical and Descriptive Account of Kachari Tribes in N.C. Hills with Specimen of Tales and Folklore*. Shillong: The Assam Secretariat Press, 1885.

Tamuli, P. and P. Sharma. "Ethno-medico-botany of the Dimasa Kachari of North Cachar Hills district of Assam." *Indian Journal of Traditional Knowledge* 9/4 (October, 2010): 718-720.

Tapadar, Zahid Ahmed, comp. *Festivals of N.C. Hills*. Haflong: Department of Information and Public Relations, N.C. Hills, Haflong, Assam, 2007-2008.

________ . *Dimasa Anvesa*. Haflong: Nikhil Bharat Banga Sahitya Sammelan, 1996.

Thachil, Jose. *The Vedic and the Christian Concept of Sacrifice*. Kerala: The Pontifical Institute of Theology and Philosophy, 1985.

Thakur, G.C. Sarma. "Religious Beliefs and Folk Deities of the Dimasa Kacharis and Karbis of Assam." In *Selected Essays on Tribes and Castes of Assam Part-1*. G.C. Sarma Thakur. Guwahati: Directorate of Assam Institute of Research for Tribals and Scheduled Castes, 2007.

Thanzauva, K. *Theology of Community: Tribal Theology in the Making*. Aizawl: Mizo Theological Conference, 1997.

Thomas, M.M. and R.W. Taylor, eds. *Tribal Awakening: A Group Study*. Bangalore: Christian Institute for the Study of Religion and Society, 1965.

Tirkey, Christopher Augustus Bixel. *Religion/Primal Religions*. Delhi: ISPCK, 1998.

Tiwari, Dinesh and Gautam Sarma. "A historical and etymological study of the Dimasa Kacharis of Dima Hasao District, Assam, India." *The Clarion* 2/2 (2013): 142-148.

Troisi, J. *Tribal Religion: Religious Beliefs and Practices among the Santals*. New Delhi: Manohar Publishers and Distributors, 1979.

Tylor, Edward Burnett. *Primitive Culture: Researches into the Development of Mythology, Philosophy, Religion, Language, Art, and Custom*. Vol. II. 4th ed. London: John Murray. 1903.

Vanlaltlani, T. *A Study of Religious Identity among the Bru of Mizoram*. Delhi: ISPCK, 2007.

________. *Tribal Religion: Mizo and Bru*. Aizawl: Mizo Theological Association, 2009.

Vashum, Yangkahao. "Sources for Developing Tribal Theology." In *An Exploration of Tribal Theology*. Edited by Wati Longchar. Jorhat: The Tzudikong Baptist Church, 1997.

Vidyarthi, L.P. and Binay Kumar Rai. *The Tribal Culture of India*. New Delhi: Concept Publishing Company, 1976.

Waardenburg, Jacques. *Classical Approaches to the Study of Religion: Aims, Methods and Theories of Research. Vol. 1, Introduction and Anthology*. Paris: Mouton, 1973.

Walling, C. Walu. *Sacrifice and Salvation in Ao-Naga Tradition: A Theological Perspective*. Impur Nagaland: C. Walu Walling, 1997.

Dictionaries and Encyclopaedias

"Sacrifice." *New Webster's Dictionary and Thesaurus of the English Language*. Edited by Donald O. Bolander, et. al. Danbury, CT: Lexicon Publications, Inc., 1992, 876.

"Worship." *The New Lexicon Webster's Dictionary of the English Language*. New York: Lexicon Publications Inc., 1988, 1135.

Bisht, Narendra S. and T.S. Bankoti. *Encyclopaedic Ethnography of the Himalayan Tribes: A-D, Vol. 1*. New Delhi: Global Vision Publishing House, 2004.

Henninger, Joseph. "Sacrifice." *The Encyclopedia of Religion*. Edited by Mircea Eliade. Vol. 12 (New York: Macmillan Publishing Company, 1987): 544-557.

The New Encyclopaedia Britannica. 1981 ed. Vol. 16. S.v. "Sacrifice", 128-135.

West, Barbara A. "Kacharis." *Encyclopedia of the Peoples of Asia and Oceania*. New York: Infobase Publishing, 2009.

Unpublished Sources

Chatry, K. K. "Significance of Agricultural Festivals of Dimasa Kacharis in Assam". M. Th. Thesis, Senate of Serampore College, 1998.

Personal Interviews

Bapui, V.L. Tluanga. Convenor, Dimasa Kachari Bible Translation, resident of Mission Compound, Haflong. Interview, 15 November 2013.

Bathari, Sajal. Resident of N.D. Razi, Haflong. Interview, 20 November 2013.

Daulagupu, K. Hojai and resident of Haflong. Interview, 19 November 2013.

Hojai, Joton. A Christian Dimasa Kachari and resident of Boildhura, Dima Hasao. Interview, 15 November 2013.

Hojai, Sarda. Former Hojai and resident of Natun Wari, Dima Hasao. Interview, 26 May 2013.

Johori, Insaan. Evangelist, resident of N.D. Razi, Haflong. Interview, 14 November 2013.

Lalsim, Ramdina. Writer and Historian, resident of Haflong. Interview, 19 November 2013.

Langthasa, Mondol. Evangelist, resident of Haflong. Interview, 17 November 2013.

Langthasa, Tarzen. Resident of N.D. Razi, Haflong. Interview, 26 May 2013.

Naiding, Denon. Resident of N.D. Razi, Haflong. Interview, 26 May 2013.

Naiding, Phonendra. A Christian Dimasa Kachari and resident of Haflong. Interview, 18 November 2013.

Ngamlai, Lalronghaka. Ex-Evangelist and Pastor, resident of Haflong. Interview, 18 November 2013.

Warisa, Palon Ch. Retired Govt. servant and resident of Sarkari Bagan, Haflong. Interview, 12 November 2013.

Government Records

District Rural Development Agency. Dima Hasao district, Assam. *Statistical Report for the year 2012*. 2012.

Inspector of Schools. Dima Hasao district, Assam. *Statistical Report for the year 2013*. 2013.

Joint Director, Health Services. Dima Hasao district, Assam. *Statistical Report for the year 2012*. 2012.

Electronic Sources

"Administration." http://nchills.gov.in/NCHILLS-ADMIN.htm (26 January 2014).

"Basic Data Sheet District North Cachar Hills (20), Assam (18)." *Government of India Census 2001*. http://www.censusindia.gov.in/Tables_Published/Basic_Data_Sheet.aspx (16 October 2012).

"Dima Hasao district." http://familypedia.wikia.com/wiki/Dima_Hasao_district (2 July 2013).

"Dima Hasao district." http://www.indianetzone.com/57/dima_hasao_district.htm (5 July 2013).

"Dima Hasao District: Census 2011 data." http://www.census2011.co.in/census/district/150-dima-hasao.html (16 October 2012).

"Dimasa Kachari people." http://en.wikipedia.org/wiki/Dimasa Kachari_people (2 July 2013).

Fernandes, Walter, Melville Pereira and Vizalenu Khatso. "Gender Impact of Tribal Customary Laws in North Eastern India: A Summary of the Final Report." http://www.onlineministries.creighton.edu (20 July 2013).

INDEX